The Myths and Legends of

BRITAIN'S PUBS

EAST *of*
ENGLAND

A Thousand Years of History and Trivia

The Myths and Legends of

BRITAIN'S PUBS

EAST *of*
ENGLAND

A Thousand Years of History and Trivia

RODNEY SIMMONDS

The Book Guild Ltd

First published in Great Britain in 2021 by
The Book Guild Ltd
9 Priory Business Park
Wistow Road, Kibworth
Leicestershire, LE8 0RX
Freephone: 0800 999 2982
www.bookguild.co.uk
Email: info@bookguild.co.uk
Twitter: @bookguild

Typeset in 11pt Minion Pro

Printed and bound in the UK by TJ Books LTD, Padstow, Cornwall

ISBN 978 1913913 236

British Library Cataloguing in Publication Data.
A catalogue record for this book is available from the British Library.

To all those wonderful people I have met in public houses.

CONTENTS

Pubs have always caught the attention of the ruling classes, either for being too abundant, too popular or, as has been the case for the past one hundred years or more, a major source of income for the treasury.

Even as far back as the dark ages they could not escape authority – in AD 965 King Edgar decreed that there should be only one beer house to each village as they had grown to such a number. He also decreed there should be only one system of measurement in the realm.

In his day people would share from a half-gallon cup called a 'Pottle'. He further decreed that these pottles should have pegs inside of them 'so no man should drink more than his share in one go'. Perhaps this was the origins of the saying 'taking someone down a peg or two'?

Surprisingly a similar custom still existed in Suffolk in the 1970s, when friends would offer each other their glasses with the salutation 'drink well, drink deep'. Later King Richard II decreed that all houses selling ale must display some form of sign so the aleconner (those unfortunate men who had to travel the countryside and towns testing the ale) would know which was an alehouse. However, an aleconner did not drink the ale to test its strength. The correct way to test it was to pour some on a wooden bench then sit on it! After a while when he stood up, how well his leather trousers stuck to the bench determined whether the ale was considered strong enough or not. Perhaps the origins of another saying – 'bench-mark'?

It was not just public houses that used signs, many others used and indeed were encouraged by the likes of King Charles I, who decreed that 'as a way these signs and posts of signs affixed to their houses and shops for the better finding out such citizens'.

Some landlords, in an effort to attract custom, had their signs hanging in the road or so low that people had to duck when passing. King Charles also decreed that the signs should be at least nine feet from the ground, so they should not be 'dangerous to the public and horse riders alike'.

Such a proliferation of signs at that time also helped people to find an address; 'the third house from the Ox Inn towards the Fleet or between the Lions Head and the shoemakers' made anyone trying to find a place easier, as house numbering of the streets was some way in the future.

Also some publicans had a second (or third) trade that they often incorporated into the pub sign, which may account for some of the more exotic names of the era.

While researching this list I have come across a number of authors who rubbish some of the more unlikely versions; I have not. Where I find a number of possibilities I have entered them all. You can choose which one to believe; I do not have the right to decide which one you should accept as true. Besides, why spoil a good story with the truth?

Some of the signs were rather strange, so much so that they would tax even the most enthusiastic crossword fanatic trying to work out what the vendor was selling. A beehive was favoured by wax chandlers but not sellers of honey; another, the death's head, was, naturally enough, a sign of an undertaker but worryingly also one for an apothecary, who also used a unicorn's head or its horn. This was presumably to indicate that their potions were as magical as the fabled beast was thought to be.

Other pub names can be quite peculiar, as you will later read. As the monarch wielded absolute power so landlords had to tread warily when choosing their pub name, although many used word trickery to get their true name on the signboard. Such as, perhaps, the innocuous Cat and Fiddle; could this be a reference to Catherine of Aragon, who was nicknamed Catherine le Fidel (Catherine the Faithful)? This is just one of a number that used word play.

To give you an idea of just how the mind worked in those days; in Ben Jonson's play *The Alchemist*, a rebus must be found for a man called Abel Drugger. It went something like this;

> He shall have A Bell – that's Abel,
> And by it standing a man called Dee

In a rug gown – that's D Rug, Drug,
And right against him a dog snarling 'er'.
That's Drugger. Abel Drugger that's his sign.
Here's no mystery and hieroglyphic.

A further category of signs were puns on the landlord's name, although sadly few of these remain, as mostly they were renamed with the change of landlord. A sign of a Hare and Bottle indicates the landlord's name was Harebottle; another showed a Hand and a Cockerel – this time the man's name was Handcock, and so on.

Then, of course there are the living signs; one landlord kept a live vulture above his entrance. Another one that was quite common at one time was a beehive complete with bees.

Some landlords went to great expense to advertise their business; one hotel at Scole near Diss in Norfolk during 1655 had a sign built so large it straddled the road and was made up of twenty-five different plates, as well as showing the arms of towns and the gentlemen of the county, along with biblical scenes and characters from mythology. The sign was reputed to have cost the landlord £1,000 to have it carved and erected – an enormous sum in those days. The sign has gone, but the hotel is still there.

After the great Fire of London in 1666, those taverns and shops that were being rebuilt were no longer allowed to have their signs jutting out into the street, but had to be incorporated into the building, being either painted or gilt or in some cases carved into the building itself. This proclamation would probably have spread throughout the land. Occasionally I have come across the remains of one, as at Tisbury near Shaftsbury.

It was not always plain sailing for the landlords, though. When the Yorkists were defeated at Bosworth Field in 1485, the victor, Henry Tudor, had a red dragon on his shield; the loser, Richard III, had a white boar, both on his flag and the supporters for his arms. After the battle there was a rush to replace the sign of the white boar by either painting it blue or replacing it with a red dragon.

Not only did a change of monarch hasten landlords to alter their signs. How many people appreciate that numerous pub names have a religious connection?

There are the obvious ones, such as the Angel and Adam and Eve, but many others have a meaning which has been largely lost, especially over the past hundred years.

The Puritans were as unpopular as they were strict, over which symbols were displayed. They became a powerful political force, especially in London and the cities.

As an example of how people felt about their strict dogma, Macaulay wrote of them, 'Puritans hate bear baiting, not because it gives pain to the bear, but because it gives pleasure to the spectators'.

For them, even some words were considered vulgar, and frowned upon, especially any which indicated people were enjoying themselves. So 'Jolly' became 'Arms' as in Jolly Carpenter, Butchers, Farmers, etc.

As a further example, 'Catherine Wheel' which commemorated St Catherine, who was put to death in the early fourth century on a spiked wheel – was changed to Cat and Wheel.

They also had their dislikes. The 'Golden Cross', a famous coaching house at the top of Whitehall, had its large cross that could only be taken down by act of Parliament – even though it was probably commemorating the final 'Eleanor Cross' nearby.

St Peter's Finger is yet a further sign connected with religion; this is thought to be the finger of the first Pope, St Peter, raised when bestowing a blessing; also the Cross Keys were the emblem of St Peter and of the Papal See in Rome.

The Hole in the Wall was quite a common name, which takes its name from Ezekiel, who said, when he looked into the hole. he 'saw every form of creeping things and abominable beasts.' I suggest, tongue in cheek, that perhaps this could have been seized on by those Puritans, but it backfired on them as it was freely taken up by landlords and customers alike, perhaps to cock a snook at them and as a joke on themselves.

While on the subject of Puritanism, they also objected to those pubs which were named after saints, as they were Catholic icons. So in some instances the landlords changed the name to flowerpot, with its innocuous flower planted in it. Many saints were symbolised with flowers (lilies for the Virgin Mary), so although they had complied with the Puritan demands, the name was, in reality, the same.

A White Horse was another biblical symbol, as told in Revelations, when Christ rides a white horse at the head of an army. The Seven Stars was a symbol of the seven-starred celestial crown worn by the Virgin Mary, who was similarly depicted in the Salutation, which showed an angel saluting her. This too was altered by the Puritans to various names such as the Soldier and Citizen or simply the Angel.

Then there is the Lamb, as in the Lamb of Christ, which is often shown with other animals, such as the Lion and Lamb. A simple rainbow is a sign of God's Covenant, as told in Genesis. A dove a symbol of the Holy Spirit.

The devil features in another sign. The Devil and St Dunstan.

Legend has it St Dunstan was busy at his craft as a goldsmith when the devil arrived and proceeded to torment him. At last becoming infuriated, the holy man took a pair of red-hot tongs from the fire, grabbed the devil by the nose and threw him into the street.

Finally in the eighteenth and nineteenth centuries the Black Swan was associated with the devil, as black was the devil's colour, which is perhaps why there are not too many called by that name.

These are just a few pub signs which have religious connotations, but of course we must remember that many years ago, long before the Reformation, monks were some of the few people who offered hospitality to the traveller, so Christian symbolism was not only important, both to them and the pilgrims, but was to be expected at a religious house.

In later days pub names were less controversial, usually intended to reflect a local trade. The Plumbers Arms, Bricklayers Arms, Carpenters Arms, etc., would often be meeting places, especially in London and other cities, when a building boom was in progress. These places were, to a certain extent, a labour exchange for those individual trades, as a builder needing a tradesman would head for that pub.

Although to change the name of a public house you must have the permission of the Justices, it was rarely refused, unless the name was thought to be offensive or some other dire reason.

Most modern names are not meant to be insulting; some are intended to reflect the past – either of the area or of the pub. Others are funny, with an eye to attracting extra custom.

Two that jump to mind as taking the rise out of landlords are; one very overweight landlord always sat on a stool to serve his customers. One of his patrons suggested – rather unkindly – he looked like an elephant on a nest. The landlord did not take offence but changed the name of the pub to 'The Elephants Nest'. The pub name has been written on the roof beams in the bar in many different languages.

Another changed the name of his pub to the 'Clock and Keys'. When asked why by customers he replied that he was the clock and his customers were the keys, because they were always winding him up. As you can see from these two examples it helps to have a sense of humour to own a pub. Oh! And when I last visited them, both were still trading.

Famous or heroic actions are also celebrated. The 'Never Turn Back' pub commemorates a famous occurrence; in November 1901 the Caister lifeboat was launched during a gale in response to flares sent up by a ship in distress. They attempted to launch the lifeboat several times, but waves were so huge it was not possible. Finally they did manage to launch; however, the lifeboat was immediately overturned and was flung back towards the beach with all twelve of the crew trapped under the hull. Only three men survived.

At the inquest the coxswain, who was one of the survivors, was asked by the coroner why they persisted with the launch in such dire conditions? His reply – "Caister men never turn back" – went into lifeboat history.

Battles are also used as pub names; possibly the landlord fought in that battle or he had other links with it, or maybe the pub opened shortly after the battle.

Corruption is a further changer of names. When Henry VIII seized Boulogne in 1544 some pubs were named 'Boulogne Bouche' after the victory. Many country people could not get their tongues round the French words, so their attempt came out as 'Bull and Bush'.

Then there is the local accent, much more pronounced several hundred years ago, when people were not so mobile as in present times. Miles from the sea you will find a pub called The Ship.

Why? When five or six hundred years ago, hardly any villager had ever seen a sailing ship. So why would they name their local pub The Ship?

But how would they pronounce the word sheep? Just a thought.

When WWI exploded it probably brought together a greater mixture of common 'Tommies' and academics than any other single circumstance in English history. The opportunity for rhyming slang, cant, regional meanings and English itself, not to mention Greek, Latin and Urdu – all ready to be distorted – was enormous, which would, and was, spread all over the country when the troops returned home.

Finally, the Greeks made their heroes into gods or constellations. The Romans feted their heroes with laurel leaves. What do the English do? They name a pub after them!

The origins of public house names, as you see, can be – and often are – shrouded in mystery.

A pub name can change at the drop of a hat, by the whim of customers, by the landlord, or corruption of the words. Some are funny; others reflect a sad event, but all were chosen for one purpose; to let the public know ale was sold at that place.

On the sad side; although I have not deliberately chosen them, many of the ones featured have closed; others are probably on the verge of doing so. This latest virus will almost certainly force the closure of marginal pubs, along with the loss, no doubt of some unique names.

The reason I have included pubs that have closed down is that this list started some years ago in a different form, so laziness dictated that I used it as a base for this book instead of starting a new one. Besides, it may bring home just how many are actually closing, along with the unique, quirky names many had and are now being lost, along with the stories that accompanied them.

Lastly there is an old joke told of the English. If a group of Italians were shipwrecked on a desert island the first thing they would build would be a church. If it were a similar group of Frenchmen, they would build a restaurant. If the group were Englishmen, what would they build? Why, a pub, of course!

I will leave you with a quote of Hilaire Belloc from his writings in the early twentieth century;

'Change your hearts or you will lose your inns and you will
have deserved to have lost them. But when you have lost
your inns, drown your empty selves, for you will have lost
the last of England.'

A fourteenth century toast:

This is what I now propose: In a tavern I shall die
With a glass up to my nose and God's angels standing by
That they may indeed declare as I take my final tot
'May God receive with loving care such a decent drunken sot.'

Taken from Liber Albus (the white book the city of London), written in 1419 by John Carpenter, the common clerk of Sir Richard Whittington, mayor of the said city.

ABBEY INN

Apart from the obvious reason for calling a pub by this name, it can often be traced back to the time when a church hospice was one of the only lodging place for pilgrims and other travellers. Most major church establishments had a hospice, especially if they were on a route taken by pilgrims.

Crowland, Lincolnshire. Haunted by a ghost of 'Old Henry', who can be heard dragging his feet across an upstairs room. Henry Girdlestone was a local farmer and Abbey regular, who in 1844 bet someone that he could walk one thousand miles in one thousand hours. Forty days later (960 hours) he had walked 1,025 miles. Who could blame him for dragging his feet after such a hike!

Named after the Benedictine Abbey at Crowland, which was founded in the eighth century when a hermit settled on the island of Croyland some years previous.

The swinging sign shows the remains of Crowland Abbey.

ADMIRAL RODNEY

He was George Brydges Rodney, 1st Baron Rodney of Stoke-Rodney, an English naval commander, 1718-1792, born in London of an old Somerset family. He joined the navy at fourteen and took part in Hawke's victory against the French of Cape Finisterre. Governor of Newfoundland from 1748 to 1752, and in 1759 as rear admiral he routed a French flotilla at Le Harve assembled to invade England. Gained victories in Jamaica, the Leeward Islands and captured islands in the West Indies on which the American contraband trade depended.

Admiral Rodney is also the name of a rose.

Wollaton, Nottinghamshire. The building was once a farmhouse on the Wollaton estate; it was a pub from 1855, probably for the estate workers, until sold to the Home Brewery in 1924 at the same time as the remainder of the estate was sold to the city of Nottingham.

A two-storey building with dormers, it is a multi-roomed pub with a public bar at the front and a part wood-panelled lounge bar at the rear. Both rooms have oak beams and stone floors.

The building is haunted by a former landlord called Tom, who was the innkeeper until 1875. Two more ghosts make an appearance on occasions; Sarah was a serving girl who delights in throwing things about in the kitchen; the other is a gentleman dressed in a 1940s-style black suit.

The swinging sign shows the admiral seated at ease.

AFFLECK ARMS

Dalham, Suffolk. A two-storey thatched Elizabethan pub which was the first building to be constructed when the village began to be settled, then of course it was a beer house. There are a number of rooms and is a 'Quiet Pub', which means *no music* only good conversation. Outside there is a rear garden and patio whilst at the front over the road there are tables and benches beside the River Kennet.

The pub takes its name from one of the last members of the Affleck family, who owned Dalham estate, while another of the relatives married an actress who was teetotal; she promptly closed the pub down 'as it was full of roughnecks and vagabonds'. Needless to say it opened up again shortly after.

Reputedly there is a ghost of a Grey Lady seen by some of the customers – perhaps after a good session?

The hanging sign shows the family crest and motto '*Pretiosum Quod Utile*' ('What is useful is valuable').

ANGEL

Immediately recognisable by everyone – the predominant holy icon. Although I have seen pubs that have placed a different attribute to the name; one such was a barmaid serving a customer with a foaming pint with the sun shining brightly through an open window.

Bury St Edmunds, Suffolk. A large eighteenth century coaching house situated almost opposite the entrance to the ruined St Edmundsbury Cathedral. It was the main coaching stop on an important crossroads north and south as well as east and west.

Charles Dickens stayed here in 1859 and 1861 when he gave readings at the nearby Athenaeum, an eighteenth century assembly hall.

It was at the Angel Mr Pickwick waited to receive news of the breach of promise action against him by Mrs Bardell.

Grantham, Lincolnshire. Properly The Angel and Royal. Originally just the Angel, the Royal being added after a visit in 1866 by Edward VII, then Prince of Wales. Story has it that a suggestion, it be called the Royal Angel was quietly vetoed, as although the prince was royal he was no angel!

One of England's oldest coaching inns on the Great North Road, the main road from London to Scotland.

It is thought to stand on the site of an even older inn where King John held his court in 1213, which was a medieval monastic hostelry originally owned by the Knights of St John of Jerusalem.

It has been suggested that it may have been an unfinished castle. The wrought-iron hanging sign showing an angel set against a castle keep with arms above lends weight to this. Some of the cellar masonry has been dated to the early 1200s and foundations are reputed to be ninth century with rumours of a link by tunnels to St Wulfram's Church and the town's market square.

The limestone front is from the time of the Wars of the Roses, 1455-1485. A visit by Richard III was the origin of the gold angel holding a crown over the ancient archway. The gatehouse is also fifteenth century; on its archway Edward III and Philippa, his queen, are carved in stone in commemoration of their visit. There is an angel holding a crown which supports an oriole window and another, rather weather beaten, is carved in a doorpost.

One of the rooms, known as the Chambre du Roi (king's room), is where Richard III, in October 1483, heard of the treachery of the Duke of Buckingham and sent for the Great Seal to sign his death warrant; a copy of his letter regarding Buckingham is displayed between the Richard III lounge and the King's Room where Charles I stayed during 1633.

As Grantham was the scene of Cromwell's first notable victory in the Civil Wars in 1643 he must have known the hostelry, as may Isaac Newton, who attended the grammar school. A later visitor was George IV.

During the early 1920s the word 'inn' was dropped and the Angel became a hotel.

An interesting custom has been carried on since the 1700s; the then landlord was one Michael Solomon, who, when he died, left forty shillings (£2) to pay for a sermon to be given in the parish church every Michaelmas Day, denouncing the sin of drunkenness.

Halesworth, Suffolk. A sixteenth century coaching and post house that has a bowling green attached.

Reputed to be haunted by the murderer John Ducker, who in 1862 killed a police officer, Ebenezer Tye, while being disturbed during a burglary. He was later hanged – the last public hanging in the county.

ANNE OF CLEVES

Anne was born in 1515, the sister of William the future Duke of Cleves, they were part of a Protestant family. Henry VIII was concerned that he needed an alliance with the Duke, as he thought that the Holy Roman Empire and Catholic France were preparing to attack England after the Dissolution of the Monasteries, as he had made himself the head of the English church.

He was persuaded by his minister Thomas Cromwell that such an alliance would be necessary. Henry was disappointed the moment he saw her. The dislike was intensified by her uncouth manners and lack of English, calling her a Flanders Mare. However, they were married during January 1540, but when the threat of attack receded they divorced in June of that year.

Melton Mowbray, Leicestershire. The building was originally constructed circa 1327 as a dwelling house for the parsons of the town. During the late fifteenth and early sixteenth century it became a house for the chantry priests – on the visit of the Bishop of Lincoln's in 1538 there were nine of them in the town!

A year later that all changed with the Dissolution of the Monasteries, which meant the King owned all church properties. He gave the house to his chancellor Thomas Cromwell, who then blotted his copybook after Jane Seymour's death by suggesting to Henry that he should marry a Flanders princess called Anne.

The old priest's house at Melton Mowbray was part of the divorce settlement, as it was no use to Cromwell because he had lost his head.

A two-storey stone-built pub next to the church, it has several buttresses supporting the front wall with, at one end, a Georgian-style bay window.

Trefoils cut into the bar front, along with panels shaped like Norman arches, give it a churchy feel, as do the church pew seating.

The swinging sign shows a full-length portrait of Henry VIII on one side. With a three-quarter-length one of Anne on the other.

AXE AND COMPASS

Heath and Reach, Bedfordshire. An eighteenth century Grade II listed building made of brick with a clay-tiled roof, which was a private house before it became a pub, possibly first licensed in 1857, when it was called the Axe and Compasses.

Inside, the largest room is the open-plan dining area, which was the old pub. This originally consisted of a very small tap room, bar, parlour and scullery. The public bar is separate, and to the rear, it is a square room without any character apart from a pair of opening windows that lead to a patio and garden, which also has a children's play area.

The pub appears to have been called the Axe and Compass(es) throughout its life, and as it was trading before reliable records were kept it is difficult to know how the name came about. One possibility is that it was frequented by foresters – as parts of the nearby Chiltern Hills are heavily wooded. Another is the combination of two licences into one pub.

Several books suggest that the Axe and Compass appear on the arms of the Company of Carpenters, but the arms I have seen are made up of a chevron and three pairs of compasses. The choice is yours.

There is nothing which has yet to be contrived by man, by which so much happiness is produced as by a good tavern or inn.

Samuel Johnson.

B

BADGER'S SETT

Cropston, Leicestershire. First called The Reservoir Hotel. Now one of a national chain selling pub food.

The inn has a rags-to-riches story behind the name. When the nearby reservoir was being constructed by Irish navvies, a local man by the name of Billy Booten set up a hut near to the Manor House in order to keep the navvies supplied with food and drink. His hut became known to the navvies as The Shant; a name probably derived from shanty, which in reality the hut was. In time Billy's enterprise flourished so well that he was able to move into the Manor House itself. It was then that the Manor House became known as the Reservoir Hotel, although locally it is still known as The Shant.

It has been called the Badger's Sett for at least fifty years; perhaps there was a badger's set nearby at one time. Being close to Charnwood Forest, this was quite a possibility.

BEAR

This was usually a medieval sign indicating bear-baiting was carried out. Alternatively it could refer to the arms of a local family who had a bear incorporated into the shield, as a number of landowners did have.

Stock, Essex. A sixteenth-century building, altered somewhat in the eighteenth then renovated in the twentieth century.

Haunted by a chap called Charlie 'Spider' Marshall, who worked as an ostler at the inn; he had a curious habit of climbing up the chimney of one bar with his pint of beer, then emerge in the fireplace in another, usually for payment of a drink. At times he would refuse to come down until he was encouraged to by some wag lighting a fire.

One Christmas Eve he climbed one chimney but never returned, although the chimneys have been swept many times since he climbed up, his body has never been found. However, his sooty shade remains at the Bear Inn.

BEDFORD ARMS

Leighton Buzzard, Bedfordshire. Once called the Corbet Arms after the local Lords of the Manor. The modern name is taken from the Dukes of Bedford, who own the nearby Woburn Abbey. Along with a large chunk of Bedfordshire!

The building is haunted by a Lady in Grey, who has been observed standing at the bottom of beds for several seconds, especially in room three.

Toddington, Bedfordshire. This pub has a sad story regarding one of its ghosts. Some years ago a sea captain returned home to find his wife and child had been murdered in the village; beside himself with grief he hanged himself in the pub. Although mostly heard clumping about, he is occasionally seen being described as a large man with a beard wearing a sailor's uniform.

There is also a cavalier who likes to stand by the fireplace in the bar leaning on a cane. He is said to be a small man wearing a red tunic and a plumed hat. Now closed and sold to a housing developer. Let's hope the ghosts remain!

Woburn, Bedfordshire. Built in 1724 by Henry Holland in the style of the nearby Woburn Abbey, a huge eleven-bays symmetrical two-storey brick building. Originally called The George – taking its name from the street on which it was built – but renamed after the family on whose estate it stands.

A former posting and coaching house with panelled rooms and at one time with stabling for a hundred horses. As there was so much stabling it must have been an important stop, possibly on the Roman Watling Street, although the modern road system belies that fact.

The pub is haunted by two shades; one is sitting by the chimney smoking, dressed in a peasant's smock and hat along with his sheepdog. The other is a tall White Lady, who appears at first as a white fog before taking shape then disappearing.

Now called the Woburn Hotel.

BEEHIVE

Grantham, Lincolnshire. The beehive at Grantham – as far as I know is unique, in as much as it has a living sign.

Since 1830 a beehive has hung in the tree outside the pub complete with occupants, who on average produce about 30-lbs of honey each year.

A sign on the pub itself reads;

> 'Stop traveller this wonderous sign to explore
> And say when thou hast view'd in o'er and o'er.
> Grantham now two rarities are thine.
> A lofty steeple and a living sign.'

BEES IN THE WALL

Whittlesford, Cambridgeshire. A beer house built in the 1770s stood on the site of what was known as Old Denny's House. In 1851 a new beer house was built by Charles Thurnall, who called it The Exhibition after the one held in London during that year.

In November 1861, the Prince of Wales came to hunt at Whittlesford and stopped at the pub for bread, cheese and beer when Stephen Macay was landlord.

The present name originated when a colony of bees took up residence in a wall of the pub around 1950. They liked the pub so much they stayed and are still there.

The hanging sign shows a brick wall with a central circle, in which there are two bees.

BELL INN

A sign everyone would recognise immediately and at one time possibly a religious sign as a place where food, drink and accommodation for travellers may be obtained.

Finedon, Northamptonshire. The oldest pub in the county dating from circa 1040 and claimed to be the third oldest in the country.

A most unusual pub apart from the historical associations. It is almost impossible to describe without going into a vast list of nonsensical architectural terms, but I will try. Basically it is two-storey of brown brick and stone with a tiled roof. It has five small gables facing the road, two at one side, three at the other of a three-storey tower with a pitched roof that stands proud of the main building. This tower houses an arched entrance on the ground floor with a bay window on the first; the second-storey window is plain. To the left is a ground-floor bay window with stone mullions; beside the window set in the wall is a niche with a statue of Queen Edith, wife of Edward the Confessor, who came from the village.

Inside are three rooms and a snug, all rooms are decorated in the *Olde Worlde* style and are very comfortable.

Stilton, Cambridgeshire. A seventeenth century inn, once an important staging post on the Great North Road, which was known to have had a huge copper sign weighing a quarter of a ton, some 560 pounds-heavy indeed; you do not want to hang about under that for long!

The village became the marketplace for the area, as horse-drawn coaches travelling in either direction usually made a stop there. Leicestershire farmers took their produce to the inn for collection and delivery by coach to London, where their cheese became known as Stilton, having been despatched from there.

The first real evidence of the cheese's existence dates back to the early eighteenth century, when a housekeeper at Quenby Hall in Leicestershire, Elizabeth Scarbrow, later the mother of Frances Pawlett or Paulet, made some. Frances Pawlett lived in Wymondham, Norfolk, where great cheese fairs were held. She became particularly skilled and sold much of her output to Cooper Thornhill, the landlord of the Bell, who, being an enterprising chap, made an arrangement with her granting his pub exclusive selling rights. He sold it at two shillings and sixpence a pound. Travellers who stopped at the inn were given the cheese for their meals, which helped spread its popularity.

First it was called Lady Beaumont's cheese, then later Quenby cheese, but gradually became known as Stilton. Where the recipe came from is unknown, but in 1727 Daniel Defoe in his *'Rides'*, more correctly *'Tour Through the Whole Island of Great Britain'*, mentioned Stilton as a town famous for its cheese, which was served with a spoon in which to eat the maggots. John Nichols, historian of Leicestershire, has, however, recorded that actually the cheese was first made at Little Dalby, some thirty miles away, by a Mrs Orton about 1730 – so what was Daniel Defoe enjoying in 1727?

Production moved from the village later that century and in 1966 the Stilton Cheese Makers' Association won a Protected Designation of Origin order, meaning cheese named Stilton could be produced only in Derbyshire, Leicestershire and Nottinghamshire.

For further consideration, we have the following: for fifteen years the residents of Stilton have been banned from making this very item, but they have now been told they can manufacture the blue-veined cheese again – so long as they do not call it Stilton. The present landlord of the Bell says this is something to celebrate after having to tell people who asked for it that it could not be manufactured legally. The Cambridgeshire villagers had been unable to do anything until a local historian, Richard Landy, found evidence the cheese really was created in the village (corroboration for this was not given). Now the Department for Environment, Food and Rural Affairs has allowed the Bell to produce the cheese for local sale. Called Bell Blue, it went on sale at this pub from 1st March, 2012.

Dick Turpin was said to visit the inn on Wednesday nights, where the most authentic DT haunting is supposed to have occurred here when in former days customers spoke of drumming hoof beats followed by the dark shadow of a rider vanishing under an archway.

Walberswick, Suffolk. A six hundred-year-old pub. For the past four hundred years the pub and the local area has been haunted by the devil in the guise of a large black dog the size of a calf, although Walberswick village is the source of many other apparitions. As a child I can remember listening avidly to an old sailor who used to take the family out fishing. He related stories not only of the black dog, but of phantom people crossing the river in a boat which would disappear halfway across. Then there is a small hunchbacked man, who visits both the pub and the church. Lastly there is the shade of a black drummer, Tobias Gill, from a local regiment, who in the eighteenth century raped and murdered a local girl. (See also the White Hart at Blythburgh.) He was hanged for the crime and now haunts the Bell, along with an angler who seems reluctant to leave the hostelry.

The hanging sign shows an old-fashioned sailor ringing a ships bell.

BELPER ARMS

Newton Burgoland, Leicestershire. Built to accommodate masons working on the church, so it is more than seven hundred years old. An extension was added about 1700. The cosy bar has low ceilings above ancient walls and open fires. Claims to be the oldest pub in Leicestershire dating from 1290, when it was called the Shepherd and Shepherdess. A phantom of regular habits glides about in the older sections, making himself felt at five minutes to four in either the afternoon or early morning. Consequently he is known as Five-to-Four Fred. His approach is heralded by a sudden drop in temperature when he roams amongst the guests, asleep or awake, accosting them with an unnerving touch.

The swinging sign shows the arms of the Belper Family.

BERNEY ARMS

Breydon Water, Norfolk. Two things that are unique to this pub, the first is you cannot drive to it: there is no road. The second is it has its own railway station, albeit about a mile away. It is a request stop but only during daylight hours as the station has no lighting. Access by foot is a hike of two and a half miles across Halvergate Marsh from the Acle straight – the road that leads to Great Yarmouth. By far the most comfortable way is by boat with the pub having plenty of moorings.

The pub closed in 2015 but at the time of writing a local community group is trying to purchase the pub. Update the pub is open as a Bistro.

The pub takes its name from Thomas Trench Berney, who owned the nearby Rheedam Cement Works.

BIRCH

Woburn, Bedfordshire. A two-storey house, only open as a pub for a few years (around 2005), although the building could be late Georgian. It seems now to be more like a restaurant. The sign shows a birch tree.

BLACK BULL

A sign every person would recognise. It may have been part of a local dignitaries shield or crest, but you must remember that black was the colour of the devil so it would be a brave – or foolhardy – person to deliberately paint anything black unless it did represent something real.

One further possibility was the price and availability of paint in the 1500s and 1600s, as the range of colours was very limited.

Balsham, Cambridgeshire. A rendered timber-framed two-storey thatched pub built circa 1660. Inside it is beamed with a polished wood floor, along with a mixture of furniture.

The road outside this pub is the haunt of 'the Shuck', described as a large dog with a bald head and wide-spaced eyes. It has a habit of jumping in front of cars only to shy away at the last moment.

Whittlesey, Cambridgeshire. Haunted by a grocer who had a shop next to the pub. It seems he hid the week's takings in his wife's washing copper but did not tell her. The following morning before he rose she had lit the copper and started her laundry, which destroyed all the money apart from some coins. He is seen in the pub, still mourning the loss of his money.

BLACK DOG

A fiend still dreaded in country places. Black dogs seem to have an affinity with ancient sites such as long barrows, standing stones and churches. Some country people believed black dogs were 'grimms' – spirits that guarded churchyards from the devil. It is possible this belief grew from the once-common practice of burying an ordinary black dog in a new churchyard on the north side, where the Devil's Door was to be found. Burial of a dog relieved any human soul from guarding the door – a duty it was believed fell to the first creature buried in a newly opened churchyard.

The devil has frequently been symbolised as a black dog.

A common name for a counterfeit or base silver coin made of pewter in the reign of Queen Anne.

It also referred to Guy de Beauchamp, Earl of Warwick, 1272-1315, who was known as the Black Dog of Arden.

Oadby, Leicestershire. First recorded in circa 1750, the pub was a coaching inn on the busy A6 road. It has a number of ghosts including an old poacher, James Hawker, who was forever boasting he would 'always poach until he died'. One night, after a particularly heavy bout of drinking, he left the pub as usual only to be found dead in a field the following day. It seemed his boast had come true!

Other ghosts are a young boy in the cellar, a groom dressed in a brown waistcoat, riding breeches and boots; and finally, a modern ghost of a man who rode his motorcycle into the wall of the pub and decapitated himself.

The pub takes its name from The Black Dog of Arden, Guy Beauchamp, Earl of Warwick, who plotted against King Edward II in 1312.

BLACK FOX

According to tradition, a black fox was thought of as an ill omen, much the same as a black dog was the bringer of ill fortune to whoever saw it.

Not so many years ago a black fox was almost as common as a red one, but because of trapping the animals for their coats they are now extremely rare.

Near Bardwell, Suffolk. When visited in 1976 there wasn't a sign outside and the building looked like a very large bungalow – which it was. The tap was some way through the building and beer was served straight from the barrel in a cellar directly behind the bar, which was a counter built of old planks sitting on bricks. This pub did not hold a spirit licence and almost certainly no longer exists. Kenny, who took me, had told me on the way there that the chap who ran the place had been an old man when he was a teenager and he was in his forties! The bar was empty of life, but Kenny shouted out of the open window and a few minutes later a very old fellow in wellington boots arrived to serve us.

We got chatting, mostly about vegetables; I later asked him if he ever got busy, to which he replied yes, that on some Saturday nights he may get ten or a dozen in the bar!

This was one of the pubs which I have been privileged to visit which was a throwback to centuries past, and what a wonderful experience it was. The seating was a school form, but no tables, and I seem to remember that a door at the back of the room (opposite the bar) led into some private quarters, as the landlord housed an extended family in the bungalow.

Near Stowmarket, Suffolk. The hanging sign showed a completely black fox. As this pub is within twenty miles of the Black Fox at Bardwell; this may be a local colour variation for Reynard. The bar was the sitting room of a house where beer was served from an enamel jug which the landlady fetched from the cellar. When we asked for bitter we were told, sorry, "we don't serve that 'ere, we only serve beer' We settled for a pint of beer which was a dark mild and tasted wonderful! This pub did not have a spirit licence and, like Bardwell, almost certainly no longer exists. Wonder if either held a licence by the 1830 Act?

BLACKSMITH'S ARMS

In the late fifteenth century three hammers appeared on the arms of the Blacksmiths' Company. As quite a number of alehouses were adjacent to a smithy, the name was, in such instances, quite appropriate.

Rothwell, Lincolnshire. Sixteenth century. Originally a blacksmiths; when changed to a pub it was first called the Nickerson Arms after a local landowner. More recently the name was changed to the Blacksmith's Arms. At one time there was a collection of flying boots donated by pilots during WWII who had to bail out.

There are two permanent ghosts in residence; one is indeed a blacksmith who sits in the bar dressed in his leather apron. The other is a farm labourer who also sits at a table with a large mug in front of him.

Other strange happenings are 1940s music emanating from the pub and the sound of wartime bombers either taking off or returning to base.

BLOCKERS' ARMS

Heads made out of wood – blockheads – are used to shape hats by workers known as 'blockers'. The term of abuse, a block head, meaning having little more sense than a hat maker's wooden block, no doubt originated from these.

It could also refer to those who made blocks for printing.

Luton, Bedfordshire. Takes its name from the fact the town was well known for the manufacture of hats up until the late '50s and early '60s. The pub was close to where the hat factories in High Town were located; it was first mentioned as licensed in 1872, although it was certainly selling beer before then – perhaps as early as 1850. It did not become a fully licensed house until about 1920.

Built either on the site of, or close to it, a pub called the Windmill, which took its name from a local windmill which blew down in a gale during the eighteenth century.

Until some time prior to WWII there was a smithy behind the pub which was numbered 5½.

The pub recently has had a chequered career, as it was damaged by arson in 1990, refurbished then closed in 1994, reopened as The Well a couple of years later, another name change to a club called the Déjà Vu, before finally closing in 2008.

BLUE BALL

As a heraldic sign it relates to the Courtenays, Earls of Devon.

Balls of various colours were often the sign of quacks or fortune tellers in days gone by.

Asheridge, Buckinghamshire. Built around 1863 of brick with flint infill on the ground floor with the first-floor tile covered. Originally called the Blue Ball but renamed the Asheridge Arms for reasons not found. It has now reverted to its old name.

BLUE BELL

Possibly a political gesture indicating the landlord – or the landowner – was either a Whig, whose colour was blue, or that the pub was used to hold political meetings. Some signs show the bluebell flower. Other signs or reasons may well be purely local, especially those around Belvoir Castle, owned by the Manners family.

Hempstead, Essex. Early sixteenth century. Originally called the Crown, reputed to be the birthplace of Dick Turpin, the notorious highwayman of the early eighteenth century, whose father was the landlord at the time.

Part of the pub at the rear was then a butcher's shop, as it appears that his father also worked as a butcher.

There is a large plaque on wall saying it was Turpin's birth place. The hanging sign shows the flower.

The story has certainly caught the imagination of the British public over the years, Turpin being associated with more pubs and inns than probably any other character in this country's folklore. Which begs the question; why did not one of the landlords inform the authorities and claim the reward?

Even though he is so famous I can only find a couple pubs of this name in England, with one in Sweden and another in Spain!

In truth, he was a surly, sordid robber, his face pitted with smallpox, whose Black Bess is as fictitious as the ride to York. This was a tale told by Victorian novelist William Harrison Ainsworth in 'Rookwood' and was actually performed by another highwayman – the favourite of Charles II – William Nevison, or Swift Nick, who rode the 216 miles in less than sixteen hours to establish an alibi in York after being accused of a robbery in London.

As far as history can show, the only time Turpin visited York was when he was escorted there to be hanged in 1739. Several other sources say as 'John Palmer' he had moved his business to York and it was there he was arrested. Even the place of his arrest is confused; some say it was at the Green (or Red) Dragon at Welton, while others tell of Brough. Whatever the truth, he was caught and hanged on the 7th April 1739 near what is now York Racecourse.

When things got too dangerous for him in and around London and Essex he decided to move to Yorkshire, where some time later he was arrested for shooting a landlord's rooster then threatening the man himself. Once arrested the magistrates began to investigate how John Palmer, as he was then known, made his money. They quickly uncovered a number of rustling charges made from farmers in nearby Lincolnshire. The final nail in his coffin, so to speak, was a letter he sent to his brother begging him to give him some sort of character reference.

However, the brother, perhaps suspecting who the letter was from and what it contained, refused to pay the sixpence postage. So the letter was returned to the post office, where the postmaster, who had been Turpin's old school master, recognised the handwriting and reported the fact to magistrates.

Once identified as the highwayman Dick Turpin his fate was sealed, although the only charge they could lay before him was horse stealing, which in any case the penalty was still hanging.

BLUE LION

Part of the arms of the Royal House of Denmark, possibly a compliment to James I's queen, Anne of Denmark, 1574-1619, mother of Charles I. Also the badge of the Earl of Mortimer.

In heraldry blue is often a representation for silver; the colour also stands for truth and loyalty.

Hardwick, Cambridgeshire. Seventeenth century building that became an inn during 1737. It is a single-storey cottage-type pub with dormer windows set in red-tiled roof, along with a smaller single-storey at one end.

Inside are flagstone floors, oak beams with the room on two levels, a fireplace at each end, along with contemporary furniture.

The swinging sign shows a blue lion rampant set in a blue shield.

BOAT

Self-explanatory; a sign usually seen by a river or the sea.

Berkhamstead, Hertfordshire. A rather cube-shaped brick-built building set on the banks of the Grand Union Canal dating from the mid-nineteenth century. The pub has a large terrace adjacent to the canal where drinkers can sit in the sun and watch others at play.

The swinging sign is a narrow boat.

BOATER

Luton, Bedfordshire. A modern estate pub, so called as Luton was a centre for straw-plaiting from the time of James I and famous for manufacture of the boater, a hard straw hat worn by men, now occasionally seen being worn by traditional butchers. The name was changed in 2011 to the Jolly Milliner, which still reflects Luton's past as a hat-making town.

BRANDY WHARF

Lincolnshire. This isolated pub is on the banks of the River Ancholme near Brigg. It is so hard to find: the best directions I can give is the post code, which is DN 21 4RU. This is now very much a cider pub selling many different ones, both on draught and in the bottle.

It takes its name not from the French brandy but from an ancient Viking tribe, the Brandes, who had settled the area. Although it is not to say that smuggled brandy was not unloaded at this isolated spot over the years, especially as it was part of the old Roman river system which linked East Anglia with Lincolnshire, so while the Revenue Cutter patrolled the sea the smugglers were free to use the inland waterways.

The swinging sign shows a man leaning on a barrel holding aloft a pint of beer or cider.

BREWERY TAP

This was generally a tavern or small pub close to a brewery in which their beer was sold.

Alternatively a tap room was another name for a public bar. 'Tap' was also the act of broaching a cask – usually by knocking a brass tap into the end of the barrel – prior to drawing liquor from it, usually several days before it was needed so as to allow the beer to settle and clear naturally.

Luton, Bedfordshire. A two-storey corner building with clapper board-cladding on the first floor of the original pub.

Opposite the Flowers Brewery (was JW Green's) on Park Street West. This corner pub was first noted as a beer house in 1894, although the building may be seventeenth century. After a fire in 1979 the 'Tap' was extended to the building next door and made into a large open-plan room that naturally divides into separate areas.

The pub did not acquire a full-on licence until 1958. Up until then it had been a beer house.

Swinging sign shows a tapster filling a jug from the barrel prior to dispensing it.

BRITANNIA

The Roman name for the parts of Great Britain which they controlled, roughly present-day England and Wales. The first known representation of Britannia as a female figure is on a Roman coin of circa AD 161. The story goes that to appease the inhabitants of England and Wales the Romans took a Celtic god, Brigantia, dressed her in flowing robes, stuck a Roman helmet on her head, gave her a spear and called her Britannia.

A figure wearing a helmet, carrying a shield and trident, subsequently appeared on English copper coin in 1672 during the reign of Charles II, the model being Frances Stewart, the Duchess of Richmond and Lennox, who refused to become one of his mistresses.

A hanging sign could also represent the Royal Yacht, which was built in Glasgow by John Brown Shipyards and commissioned in 1953. It has since been de-commissioned and resides at Edinburgh as a tourist attraction.

Kegworth, Leicestershire. At the back is an old stockingers' cottage (one who knits stockings) which was used for that until 1956. Not clear if this is/was part of the inn.

BRITISH FLAG

Usually the Union flag is on the sign.

Harwich, Essex. First appeared on records as a beer house in 1873 but could well have been a beer house before that under the 1830 licensing act which allowed Customs and Excise to licence any household to open up for the sale of beer for the princely sum of two pounds. The sale of alcohol was officially limited to beer but, as is told in later pubs, this rule was more often than not bent with under-the-counter sales – especially of contraband. It retained its beer-only licence until 1953, when the brewery owner purchased a full licence for reputedly, according to one source, the sum of £2,000 – an amount that is hard to believe, as the building itself would not be worth that much.

The pub is two storey with a pair of dormers in the roof, built of mellow red/brown bricks, it is a Grade II listed building.

The swinging sign shows the British Lion, the Union Flag and the Royal Standard on one side of the sign, with the name on the other.

BROCKET ARMS

Ayot St Lawrence, Hertfordshire. Opposite the church is a Tudor black-and-white cottage flanked at one end by this fourteenth century half-timbered and white-washed pub owned by members of the Brocket family, whose hall is nearby.

Interior is original, with low beams, lanterns, inglenook and stone-flagged floors. The building was first used as the monastic quarters for the Norman church until the Reformation. Said to be haunted by a monk who, so the legend goes, was tried and hanged here. Sightings have described him as 'affable'- surprising, considering his end.

George Bernard Shaw moved into the old rectory in the village in 1906 and was surely a visitor to the inn, as it was only a five-minute walk away.

At one time Sunday school used to be held in the tap room.

The swinging sign shows the coat of arms for the family, with the motto 'Felis Demuleta Mitis'. which translates as 'Gentle in Peace, Fearless in War'.

BULL

A sign everyone would recognise and one with a number of reasons behind the name.

Sometimes corrupted from La Boule (Latin: *bulla*), the seal of a collegiate body or monastery, the sign associating an inn or hostel with the religious house responsible for it.

Some pubs with this name can be traced back to the Reformation, when following the annulment of his marriage to Catherine of Aragon, Henry VIII rejected the Catholic faith. His defiance of the Pope and the Papal Bull threatening him with excommunication is displayed as a bull's head on his coat of arms. Later other landlords changed their signs to the four-legged type to avert the religious persecution which was all too likely.

Pub signs consisting of a plain (or coloured) bull, which may perhaps be a reference to the cognisance of the house of Clare, and to Richard, Duke of York.

Bull-baiting was popular until Parliament passed a law forbidding it in 1835. Its popularity would account for the bull as a sign being found in the centre of many market towns. Usually the bull was tethered to a ring in the market place and dogs set upon it, as it was thought that a baited animal was more tender.

Bulling the barrel; was pouring water into a rum cask when it is nearly empty to prevent it from drying out and leaking. The water, impregnated with the spirit and very intoxicating, was known as 'bull'.

Long Melford, Suffolk. Dates from circa 1450 and possibly a cloth merchant's house when the village was a settlement for Flemish weavers.

It has been an inn since 1570; later the principal posting house in the town during the coaching era. It serviced the main road between London and Norwich.

In 1935 a one hundred-year-old brick front was removed, which exposed timberwork revealing one of East Anglia's finest mediaeval buildings.

A haunting is attributed to the murder in 1648 of a yeoman named Richard Everard carried out in the hallway by a certain Roger Greene. They had been arguing over politics, but tempers rose, then Greene pulled a knife and stabbed Everard. The ghostly victim has been seen lying in the hall covered in blood; witnesses who ran for help were astounded to find on their return… no body.

The large oak door to the dining room off the hall is known to swing open by itself and several objects have been seen to fly across the room, one witness having to duck to avoid a copper jug which came at him. Chairs there have been moved mysteriously overnight, although having been left in their usual places at closing time. A previous landlord spoke of footsteps passing his room at night but always found the corridor empty. Hardly convinced of there being nothing there, he brought his dogs upstairs to continue looking, but on reaching the passage they refused to go further, becoming cowed and growling. Another guest, as there was a rap on the door, expected her morning pot of tea. When she called out, "Come in!", there was a resounding crash. Going to the door expecting to find smashed china, she found no one there, nor any sign of wreckage.

Stony Stratford, Buckinghamshire. This and the Cock Inn opposite are credited with the origins of the saying 'a cock and bull story', as the locals of these two pubs each tried to outdo each other with wild and wonderful tales bordering on the absurd.

As coaches going in different directions stopped at each inn, this gave added fun to the story-telling.

BULL AND DOG

Sleaford, Lincolnshire. A two-storey terraced building which had a couple of dormer windows in the roof and a plaque on the wall dated 1689, showing a bull being baited by several dogs and the initials BRM in the date. The last reported baiting in the town was in 1807, the sport was made illegal in 1835 under the Prevention of Cruelty to Animals Act.

Formerly called the Black Bull. The swinging sign shows the name with Est 1995 on an orange background.

A very unusual name for a pub.

BURGHLEY ARMS

Bourne, Lincolnshire. Formerly a private house, in the market-place, where Lord Burghley, Sir William Cecil was born. He later became a statesman and founder of the Cecil fortunes, becoming Lord High Treasurer to Elizabeth I, being created Baron Burghley in 1571.

It has been an inn since about 1717, when it was called the Bull and Swan, later to become just the Bull, until the present name was adopted in 1955.

A lovely symmetrical building that has a central semi-arched doorway with leaded glass, mullioned windows on either side. May have been much larger at one time, especially if it had been a coaching house.

The swinging sign shows the arms of the Burghley family.

> Whoe'er has travelled life's dull round,
> Where'er his stages may have been,
> May sigh to think he still has found
> The warmest welcome at an inn.

Written at an inn at Henley in Arden, Warwickshire:
William Shenstone, 1714-63

CAP AND FEATHERS

The origins of this name may never be known. In medieval times during the year people dressed in their finery for Saints' Day feasts; this could be one reason for the name. Another could be that it was a pun on Tom of Bedlam, who also dressed in finery, or perhaps it was a prize for some competition: then lastly it may have been a whim of the landlord or customers.

Tillingham, Essex. Reputed to originally be a twelfth/thirteenth-century pilgrim's lodging house. In the sixteenth century the tithe of the whole village was given over to St Paul's Cathedral, possibly when good King Hal was having his tantrum with Rome. At about the same time it became the village pub.

The swinging sign is a double-sided one; a cap with a half-empty pint on a table by a window is one; the other shows two men shooting with two dogs. Understand? Me neither! This sign may have been the replacement for a previous one which the parish council objected to, as in the background it showed two dogs mating. Seems a little petty to me!

CARNARVON ARMS

The ancestral home of the Earls of Carnarvon is at Highclere, which contains mementoes of the fifth earl, who in 1922, together with Howard Carter while digging in the Valley of the Kings at Luxor, discovered the tomb of Tutankhamun, the last of the 18th Dynasty Pharaoh.

Carnarvon died two months later, his death being linked to the 'Curse of Tutankhamun' in the popular press and in people's minds.

Sutton Bonington, Nottinghamshire. Four centuries old. Reputedly haunted by the Earl and DH Lawrence, who lived in the village.

CARPENTERS ARMS

The arms of the Worshipful Company of Carpenters was founded in 1271; it was given its Royal Charter in 1477. The arms are an inverted chevron with three pairs of compasses; two above the chevron, one below, with the motto 'Honour God'. The French term for 'rafter' is *chevron* and the charge may be meant to represent a roof support.

The difference between a joiner and a carpenter is that a carpenter used nails to hold the wood together whilst a joiner used joints and glue.

Harlington, Bedfordshire. First licensed in 1790, this Grade II listed pub was first a coaching house; although it is difficult to see on a modern map which route was taken. When the railway built a station just down the road, as with so many other such inns, that trade dried up.

The pub takes its name from the first landlord – who was a carpenter by trade. Not the more usual heraldic coat of arms but a pair of human arms holding a square against a block of wood.

Stewkley, Bedfordshire. A sixteenth century mellow brown-brick inn with red/brown-tiled roof.

Here two spooks want to fight each other; one being a monk in a black habit; the other is a man dressed in grey. The kitchen also has its ghost; a woman can be seen through the window working at a table; whenever anyone enters the room she looks up and smiles before disappearing.

The hanging sign shows the traditional coat of arms for carpenters.

CARTWRIGHT ARMS HOTEL

The Cartwright family, owners of Aynho Park, lived at Cartwright Hall from

1615 to 1954, when the last squire and his son were killed in a motoring accident. The parkland, originally landscaped by Capability Brown, is now farmed and the house made into flats.

Aynho, Northamptonshire. This large rambling hotel, which was built circa 1500 from local stone, was a former coaching house on the Bicester to Banbury road.

Aynho was known as 'Apricot Village', as at one time tenants paid their cottage rents to the Lord of the Manor partly in apricots from trees provided originally by the Cartwright family. Several older houses still have these trees, many situated on the chimney wall as heat from the flue would help keep frosts away. As well as apricots, peaches grew very well there.

The swinging sign showed the coat of arms of the Cartwright family.

Last time I drove through Aynho most of the old gnarled trees had gone, but it looked as if new ones had been planted.

CASE IS ALTERED

Several explanations are given for the origin of this – you can take your pick from the stories.

A catchword in Wellington's day, the Iron Duke himself is said to have used the expression when the fortune of war changed in his favour.

Another story tells of an inn on the site of a former nunnery at Woodbridge, Suffolk, was where a Father Casey used to take confessions. Being a persecuted Catholic priest deprived of his church, he set up an altar in the inn, so Casey's Altar became garbled into 'case is altered'.

Another possible source: Edmund Plowden, the great lawyer, a Catholic under Queen Mary, was defending a fellow Catholic accused of attending Mass performed by a layman. When impeached for so doing, the layman was asked by Plowden if it was he who officiated and, when told it was, asked, "'And are you a priest?'". to which the man replied, "'No!'" Plowden turned to the tribunal, saying, "'The case is altered, for it is an axiom with the church: no priest, no Mass.'"

The more probable reason seems to be that it stems from the Spanish *Casa Alta*, meaning 'high house', a name brought back by soldiers returning from the Peninsular War. There being several other pubs in the country with this name would lend credence to this view, particularly if built in a commanding position.

It is also an early comedy by Ben Jonson, written in 1609.

One further possibility is that something may have changed in the pub; one example is the landlady got married and changed the name because of her marriage; another is a change of landlord, particularly if the pub had been run down.

Bentley, Suffolk. Date unknown but extant in 1844 when the landlord was one Phillip Burch.

There is more than one choice, though. Legend says the pub was once held by a genial landlady none too fussy about payments for beer, but when she married, her husband was not of the same mind and the case was altered. Alternatively: the original pub stood further down the lane away from the main road, so to attract passing trade, a nearby house was taken over and altered to become the present pub. During extensive changes, evidence of bricked-up doors and windows was uncovered, so either happening could account for the name.

The pub at present is community-owned by over two hundred members. It was bought in February 2014 and opened April the same year, with volunteers doing everything from painting to bar staff; however, in 2015 professional kitchen and management were recruited although volunteer bar staff still operate.

A fine sign depicts what looks to be a happy gathering seated at a table outside the inn, which is rather appropriate under the circumstances.

CASTLE

The Castle being part of the arms of Spain, so the sign may have denoted that Spanish wines could be obtained within.

Another possibility may be a corruption of Castile, as Eleanor of Castile was the wife of Prince Edward, who accompanied him on the Seventh Crusade. On returning to England following the death of his father, Henry III, he became Edward I and she his Queen. They were crowned in August 1274 at Westminster Abbey.

When Queen Eleanor died in 1290 at Nottingham, the King had erected at every overnight stop which the cortege bearing her body halted on its journey to London, a stone cross known as the Eleanor Crosses, some of which are still standing.

Also travellers could find food and shelter at some castles of the nobility, the lower hall being open to them while the upper was reserved for more auspicious guests.

Colchester, Essex. Built circa 1690, although the present two-storey building is mostly eighteenth century and typically Georgian. It is a Grade II listed building and takes the name from the nearby castle.

During a refurbishment in 1986, four skeletons from the thirteenth century were found, then it was further discovered that the building had been constructed on a Saxon burial site.

At one time the Castle was one of the main coaching houses in Colchester, situated as it is at the very centre of town.

The hanging sign shows Colchester castle.

St Albans, Hertfordshire. During the Battle of St Albans on 22nd May, 1455, the Lancastrian Duke of Somerset was killed on the steps of this inn.

The legend tells that he had previously been warned by soothsayers to avoid castles; he was diligent in observing the advice, avoiding staying in castles. However, he was killed by Richard Plantagenet at an alehouse, the sign of the Castle.

> For underneath an alehouse' paltrey sign, The Castle in St Albans,
> Somerset hath made the wizard famous in his death – Sword
> hold thy temper; heart, be wrathful still: Priests pray for enemies,
> but princes kill.

Henry VI, Part 2, Act V, Scene 2

CASTLE AND FALCON

This is a somewhat mysterious sign. One reference states that it was the crest of Catherine Parr, the last wife of King Henry VIII, but I can find nothing to substantiate this claim.

A Falcon, apart from being a bird of prey, was a small-bore cannon with a two and half inch bore which would be used against advancing infantry, but, of little use against a castle during a siege.

The last two possibilities are that it was a combination of two pub names whose licences were handed in to get one new one. Or a landlord had moved pubs and added his old pub name to the new one so any of his old customers would know where he was. This was probable in a city but most unlikely in a small town such as Newark. So it's up to you.

Newark, Nottinghamshire. The swinging sign shows a Falcon with a castle in the background.

CHEQUERED SKIPPER

Ashton, Oundle, Northamptonshire. The pub was built at the turn of the twentieth century from a design possibly of William Huckvale for Charles Rothschild; it was originally called the Three Horseshoes. Made of stone with a thatched roof, this Grade II listed building suffered fire damage in 1990 but has been rebuilt to a very high standard – some say even better than the original.

Inside the bar boasts a flagstone floor, light oak beams and a stone bar; there is a dining room and a functions room which is a converted barn, complete with roof beams, trusses, along with hay racks on the wall in case you fancy a little grazing in between courses.

The Annual World Conker Championships are held on the green outside the pub on the second Sunday in October, with some contestants playing in fancy dress or adorned with conkers, other players come from as far afield as Australia.

The swinging sign is of course, a butterfly, but this one is made entirely of coloured nails.

CHEQUERS

One of the earliest decorations. Chequered boards found in the ruins of Pompeii are believed to have indicated draughts or a game similar could have been played.

There are several options for the origins of the chequer board, although all agree it was used to keep track of monies. Some say it was originated by the Romans; others, that it was from the Norman or Plantagenet Kings.

The treasury table was covered with a checked cloth. Then, with the aid of coloured counters, revenues were calculated. Not only was it the treasury which used a chequered cloth or board; a multitude of other reasons could be indicated. Several families had a chequered shield as part of their coat of arms; the Fitzwarren family, whose head in the days of Edward IV was invested with the power of licensing vintners and publicans, was one. Houses licensed by him often displayed the Fitzwarren arms; these were chequers of *or* and *gules* (gold and red). They were often corrupted to 'Red Lattice'. A red lattice at the doors and windows signified that an alehouse was duly licensed. In some cases the 'lattice' was further perverted into 'lettuce', and the colour of the alternate checks into green. Such a sign used to be in Brownlow Street, Holborn.

A chequer board could be another way of informing customers that an inn provided a banking service – perhaps explaining why so many pubs called 'The Chequers' were found in seaports, which would have had a succession of cosmopolitan visitors.

The chequer board was part of the coat of arms of the first Earls of Warrené and Surrey, whose colours were gold and blue.

In some cases payment of doles etc. were made in public houses and a chequer board was provided for the purpose, and so the sign came to indicate a house where parish authorities met for that and other purposes.

The sign could also announce to strangers that games may be played there, offering diversions such as 'kettle-noddy-boards, truncks, billiards, fox-and-geese and shovel-board or shove-groat, a game similar to shove-ha'penny'.

Amersham, Buckinghamshire. This pub is thought to be haunted by some of the Lollard Martyrs, who were followers of John Wycliffe, the man who had translated the Bible from Latin into English two centuries before. To read it in another language other than Latin was considered heresy, with a punishment of being burnt at the stake. One story tells that the seven martyrs spent their last night upstairs in the pub before being escorted by a warder named Osman to their deaths. A grim rider to the story of the burnings is that a daughter of one of those to be burnt, Joan Clerke, was forced to light the faggots on which her father stood.

A number of hooded figures have been seen in the pub over the years, although no one can be certain exactly who they were.

Anstey, Hertfordshire. In a pit west of the village is a dark recess known as Cave Gate, said to be the entrance to a tunnel claimed to extend half a mile to Anstey

Castle. Despite much talk in the Chequers tavern, many years ago no one dared explore it. One day the pub's old fiddler, Blind George, agreed to venture in for a bet. Taking his dog with him, he entered Cave Gate, fiddling as he went so those following could hear him as they walked on top of the tunnel behind the music which, halfway to the castle, ceased. A shriek rent the air, followed by silence. Those tracking George ran back to Cave Gate in time to see his dog come rushing out howling and tailless, with its hair singed. The Blind Fiddler was never seen again and the villagers decided to block up the passage.

According to some, the course of the tunnel is still plain, as when snow settles it melts first along its route. This tale was documented in 1903 but thought to have had originated before the turn of the nineteenth century, one elderly customer having remembered his grandfather telling him the tale as if it had taken place even longer before that.

Church records show Anstey did indeed have a fiddler named George, but he was buried in the churchyard, not somewhere subterranean and unknown.

The tunnel is still there, but it penetrates no further than thirty feet from the Gate, and the far end of the tunnel is actually the old route for the water supply to Anstey Castle.

The pub is now called the Blind Fiddler with a sign of an outline of a fiddler in black on a light background.

Similar tales have been told at Granchester, Binham Priory in Norfolk and Richmond Castle, Yorkshire. There are others all over the country.

Fowlmere, Cambridgeshire. At least four hundred-year-old coaching inn where some time ago a child's shoe, a piece of iron and a sliver of bone were found behind the fireplace. This was quite a common practice at one time, to ward off evil spirits and as a charm against fire.

This pub was employed for a most unusual use for a public house – in fact it has been the only one I have come across since starting this list; it was a chapel of rest for coffins travelling between London and Cambridge.

Needless to say, it is haunted. Not, as one may think, by those being conveyed in coffins, but of by persons who did the transporting. Over the years three of those who carried the coffins have died at the pub and remain to this day as spirits.

They say stranger things happen at sea. I'm not sure of that!

Regularly visited by Samuel Pepys when he visited his uncle and family at their farm at Brampton.

Friday Bridge, Cambridgeshire. A two-storey brick-built cottage-type pub with a red-tiled roof.

There is a story regarding the ghosts that haunt this pub; it seems that about three hundred years ago a group of men held an all-night game of cards in the pub. During the game one man died.

While he was lying in the church awaiting burial the others decided to have one more game over his body before he was buried. As they dealt the cards they were struck by lightning and were all killed; since then they have haunted the Chequers with loud moaning. There are also the sounds of children laughing and running up and down a corridor.

St Albans, Hertfordshire. Situated near the Cross Keys. On 17th February, 1461, it was between these inns the Yorkists forced an entry into the town, blowing trumpets and shouting their war cry; "A-Warwick! A-Warwick!" This was second battle of the town, sounds of which are still sometimes heard as reported in *The Folklore of Hertfordshire* by Doris Jones-Baker.

Westoning, Bedfordshire. Parts are perhaps seventeenth century, a timber-framed structure with brick infill and thatch. To quote Bedfordshire County Council's description, 'it is a Grade II listed building of special interest. The building has a single storey with attics at the front with two storey's at the rear which is actually earlier'.

The original building was first recorded when John Woodward left it to his son in 1797 when it may have been called the Griffin. Records show that there was a further pub called The Bell opposite The Chequers, but by 1828 it was the only pub in the village. Since then another pub also called the Bell opened up further down the road.

The hanging sign did show two men in long wigs, smoking churchwarden pipes and playing the board game, but I see now that it has changed to black-and-white squares on a shield with the motto '*Onore in Servzio*' ('Honour on Duty').

CHIMNEY CORNER

Kempston Hardwick, Bedfordshire. This early twentieth century pub was probably built to serve the workers from the nearby London Brick Company. The name alludes to the many factory chimneys which at one time could be seen from the pub; most were demolished in the 1990s. The name is unique in the world.

The sign shows a man wheeling a barrow of newly made bricks.

Update; at the time of this review, the pub is closed.

CHRISTOPHER INN

The legend goes that Christopher carried an unknown child across a river who, when on the other side, reveals himself to be Christ – so he became the patron saint of travellers. A sign such as this in days when people walked everywhere would have been a welcome sight, as they would hope for a welcome, hot food and good beer.

Eton, Buckinghamshire. A coaching house has been on this site since 1511, although the current building is more recent. Possibly having a Georgian façade added some time in the late eighteenth or early nineteenth century.

During the reign of King Charles II, Major George Sydenham often discussed religion and the immortality of the soul with his friend Captain William Dyke. They made a pact that whoever died first would appear between twelve and one in the morning at the summerhouse in Captain Dyke's garden three days after the funeral. The Major died first and Captain Dyke went there at the appointed time, but Sydenham did not appear.

About six weeks later Captain Dyke and his cousin, Dr Thomas Dyke, put up at the Christopher Inn in order to place his son at the college, where they stayed for several nights. The morning before returning to Somerset, the captain remained in his bedroom longer than normal, so the doctor went to investigate; when he did his cousin's eyes were staring and he was trembling all over. He told the doctor he had seen the major in his room at the inn; just after daybreak the major had drawn the curtains then apologised for not being able to turn up at the appointed time but had come now to tell him there was a God, 'a very just and terrible one so you'd better turn over a new leaf'. The ghost then had picked up a sword from the table – which he had given to his friend as a gift – drew it and commented on its rusty appearance, then, shortly after, vanished. From that day the captain was a changed man. He died two years later.

COACH AND HORSES

Such a sign indicated a posting or coach house before the era of the dreaded internal combustion engine. It also may have indicated to independent travellers that stables and a coach house could be hired for the night.

Ashby St Ledgers, Northamptonshire. Originally a sixteenth century farmhouse to which a Victorian façade was added in 1892. It was not very graciously modernised in the 1960s, but later owners have redeemed much of this, having uncovered original inglenooks and stone floors which, thankfully, had not been removed. The lounge bar has traditional furnishings, plenty of brass and a log fire, while old pub games can be enjoyed in the front bar.

The Gunpowder Plot was hatched here as well as at nearby Althorp Hall.

Kibworth Harcourt, Leicestershire. Hereby hangs a tale of the miller of Kibworth Mill. As a wager at a celebration in the Coach and Horse [sic], he made a bet to drink a certain number of gins. In an effort to make him lose, his cronies made them doubles, but he managed them all, thus winning his bet, only to fall down unconscious. Later he was pronounced dead and put in a coffin. Although noises were supposedly heard from the coffin, no one bothered to investigate and he was duly buried. (All of them could only have been as drunk as he was.) A suspicion prevails he had been buried alive, as afterwards his ghost was regularly seen.

COCK

This has many derivations. As the Biblical emblem relating to St Peter (he who denied Jesus three times before the cock crowed), it adorns many towers and steeples of churches in the guise of a weathercock.

It was the warlike emblem of the Goths and therefore used in Gothic churches for ornament.

The bird was dedicated to Apollo, the sun god, as it announces the rising sun and there is also the more obvious reference to cockfighting.

A cock horse was an extra mount attached at the head of a four in hand to assist going up a hill, and many signs reflect this. It was also the name applied to a small horse particularly suitable for a lady and was also another name for the spigot or tap on a barrel.

Cock ale was a type of beer popular from the sixteenth century flavoured with spices and… a cockerel. A canvas bag with dried fruit and spices, along with a well-cooked cockerel that had been mashed in a mortar and pestle, were added to a quantity of ale. After a week or so you should bottle it then give it time to ripen before drinking. Recipes vary; some advise seeping the mashed cockerel in sack, and the spices and fruit can differ.

Broom, Bedfordshire. A two-storey brick structure with one gable end at right angles to the other. It became a licensed beer house in 1836, although the building is older, having been sold during 1829 by the Third Baron Ongley of Old Warden as a residential cottage.

In 1860 when offered at auction it was described as 'an old well-established beer house known as the Cock and Tuns'. By 1903 it had become known simply as The Cock.

This two-room pub, which is a Grade II listed building, has quarry-tiled floors throughout with pine-panelled walls, cupboards and built-in settles. It is on CAMRA's National Inventory of Historic Pub Interiors and is described as 'a rare and unusually complete nineteenth century rural pub which has its interior complete'.

Known as 'the pub with no bar', as real ales are served from casks racked by the cellar steps. There is also a quirky wood and leather skittles set arranged as a chair.

Outside there is the compulsory garden overlooking the Bedfordshire countryside. The swinging sign shows a cockerel in all his magnificent plumage.

Henham, Essex. Built circa 1547 and licensed since 1620. It was a coaching inn where Nell Gwyn once stayed when Charles II visited the nearby more luxurious George Hotel.

Over the years landlords have noticed that paranormal activity increases whenever there is building work being carried out on the pub. One licensee, aware of this, laid on vases of flowers and spoke to the ghosts, assuring them that whatever was being done would be an improvement. It worked! For some years the spirits stayed quiet, that is until the next lot of work is carried out.

The most often-seen ghosts are a cavalier in Civil War uniform and a serving girl with a rather low-cut dress.

Sibson, Leicestershire. Claimed as being one of the oldest inns in England, built about 1250, although there is no documented evidence of its having been used as such earlier than 1821. A local historian described it as 'a delightful thatched brick and black timber building of the sixteenth or seventeenth century with perhaps traces of an earlier one'.

An historic connection can possibly be made with Richard III, as Bosworth Field was but a few miles from the village, with King Dick's Well being at Shenton, where the King is said to have taken his last drink before losing his crown in a thorn bush. Crown Hill, not far from Sibson, is where, once retrieved, the crown was put on the head of Henry Tudor. If the inn was extant in those times, who's to say none of the royal party didn't nip in for a swift half – either before or after the battle?

Another royal visitor suggested is Queen Elizabeth I on her way to Tutbury Castle to visit the imprisoned Mary Queen of Scots. This might not be tenable, as it is known the queens never met, but she might have got this far and then changed her mind,

An earlier date for the pub is the 1730s is suggested, due to a connection with Dick Turpin. Information in the pub says the highwayman would go there after 'working', taking refuge in the bar chimney and stabling his horse in the cellar. After a career in Essex where he was born, Turpin had moved to Leicestershire, as gradually his gang members were caught. He is said to have lived in a cottage with his parents near Watling Street, not far from Sibson.

If, as is thought, the Cock was owned by the church until 1934, this would hardly have been approved of by the godly – if they had ever known.

There is Turpin memorabilia in the bar and outside is a mound said to have been used for cock-fighting – hence the name of the pub.

Stony Stratford, Buckinghamshire. One of the most famous of coaching inns on the London to Manchester road where passengers were allowed a halt of less than half an hour in which to demolish dinner. Charles Dickens may have been a visitor, as he is thought to have based Mr Turveydrop in *Bleak House* on a local dancing tutor. The other half of the 'Cock and Bull' saying.

COCK AND BELL

Derived from the custom in parts of the country of having cockfights on Shrove Tuesday; being the last feast day before Lent, the loser would finish up in the pot. The owner of the cock which had won the most fights was awarded a small silver bell to be suspended from a button on his hat for three successive Sundays.

Long Melford. Suffolk. A sixteenth century inn which is a timber-framed house that has a bar and two dining areas, one of which has been a cockpit; there is also a function room with a bar.

Hanging sign shows a cockerel standing on a bell.

COCK AND RABBIT

Great Missenden, Buckinghamshire. The original pub on the village green was Elizabethan; in 1900, members of the Liberty family bought the village, but noise from the inn was not to their liking, so another was built away from the manor house on the other side of the green. There is no mention of the original building being demolished, so if not, it may now serve a different purpose. The new pub has a panelled lounge with open fires and a large garden. Latterly, both the landlord and the food served are Italian.

It is the only known pub with this name. It also has a weather vane with a running rabbit and a cockerel on the top of the vane.

The swinging sign shows a cockerel and a rabbit cut out in silhouette.

COCK O' THE NORTH

George, 4th Duke of Gordon, 1770-1836, who raised the Gordon Highlanders in 1794, as head of the clan his traditional epithet was Cock o' the North.

There are several other possibilities for the name; a traditional bagpipe tune whenever the Gordon Highlanders march. It is also a name given to a railway locomotive and a dialect word for Brambling.

Hatfield, Hertfordshire. It seems to have been built in 1936, although the history is not clear, nor is any connection with the Gordon clan. The rail locomotive was built in 1934, so that could be the best bet.

A large road house on the Great North Road with plenty of places for privacy and log fires.

The swinging sign shows the words in red with yellow shadow on a purplish background with a three-dimensional crowing cock mounted on top of the sign.

COMET

Hatfield, Hertfordshire. This pub commemorates the De Haviland Comet aeroplane produced at Hatfield.

The pub was built in 1933, designed as an Art Deco building by E. B. Musman in the shape of an aircraft which has a two-storey projecting centrepiece with a rounded end and wings on either side.

Until the 1950s the sign depicted the De Haviland DH 88, also known as the Comet, a wooden monoplane racer named Grosvenor House, famous for its distinctive pillar box red colour. The aircraft was the winner the 1934 MacRobertson Cup air race from England to Australia. Covering the 11,300 miles from Mildenhall in Suffolk to Melbourne in seventy hours fifty-four minutes and twelve seconds, the record still stands for piston engine aircraft to this day. The actual aircraft is part of the Shuttleworth collection housed at Old Warden airfield.

This aircraft gave De Haviland experience in building wooden aircraft, culminating in the manufacture during WWII of the Mosquito bomber.

There is no swinging sign, but a model of the DH 88 is on a plinth instead.

COMPASSES

Greenfield, Bedfordshire. A two-storey brick building, the first mention was in 1854 when it was a beer house, a situation which remained until 1951, when it applied for and was granted a full licence.

At one time there was a slaughter house and butcher's shop as part of the premises, as well as stabling for two horses.

This is a traditional village pub with a lounge and, a bar with an open fire. Outside there is a garden with disabled access at the side of the building.

An unusual swinging sign showing three types of compass: a ship's, a pair of drawing compasses, and dividers.

COOK'S FERRY INN

Chingford, Essex. There have been at least two pubs on the site; the first was built around 1768, which was a large square Georgian building; the second was, I think, built in the 1950s.

Named after the family which once ran the ferry across the Lea Navigation river. One, Matthew Cook who lived in the nineteenth century, was an eccentric who had fourteen cats which accompanied him on his crossings, not always to the delight of his passengers.

COOPERS ARMS

Commemorates the Coopers' Company dating from the early sixteenth century. Coopers were makers of wooden barrels, casks and tubs.

Hitchin, Hertfordshire. The original stone-built building with a tiled roof dates from the mid-fifteenth century, when it was a courtyard building; today only the south and west wings remain. Probably a coaching house, as Hitchin was at the crossing of two major roads – the Great North Road and the Icknield Way.

Inside there are exposed beams, a beautiful carved fireplace with wood burner and two resident ghosts; one is a white cat who walks into the bar then disappears through a wall; the other a one-legged monk who 'floats' about before he too disappears.

Strangely, although the pub is called the Coopers Arms it was once the Guild Hall for the Tilers.

The hanging sign shows the Coopers Arms with underneath their motto, 'love as brethren'.

CORK AND BULL

Luton, Bedfordshire. Haunted by a murdered girl called Ann who dresses all in white. The unusual thing about Ann is she talks and even touches visitors who do not realise she is a spirit.

Another name of which the origins are lost with the passage of time.

COWPER'S OAK

Weston Underwood, Buckinghamshire. The nearby lodge was at one-time, the home of the poet William Cowper, 1731-1800, who wrote 'The Yardley Oak', verses about a tree in Yardley Chase. This gives its name to this inn.

The building is an early nineteenth century wisteria-covered brick building that has a small front terrace and a big orchard at the rear. Inside there are wooden floors, bare stone round the open fire and painted panelling.

The swinging sign shows the venerable oak leaning slightly (perhaps it had called in for a quick one) but in full leaf.

CROMWELL COTTAGE

One of the few references to dear old Ollie of Civil War Fame. Before the Battle of Naseby the parliamentary troops were stationed in the village under General Fairfax; Cromwell joined them on 13th June, 1645, so the pub name commemorates the occasion.

Kislingbury, Northamptonshire. The stone building was a farmhouse until about 1820, when it was divided into three cottages; what year it became a pub is not clear, but inside it has modern furnishings on a polished wood floor while retaining character beams and open fires.

The swinging sign show the head and shoulders of OC himself, this time without the warts!

CROOKED BILLET

A billet was a requisition requiring accommodation for military personnel, civilians evacuees, etc, which came to refer to any lodgings. A crooked billet was, in soldiers' slang, not a very good one. A billet was also a thick length of wood, usually used for burning.

Kingswood, Buckinghamshire. A huge contemporary-designed pub which is on Akeman Street, the ancient Roman road, now the A41, which connected Watling Street with the Fosse Way.

This pub has a very special ghost; she is reputed to be the 'Fair Rosamund', the mistress of King Henry II who was supposed to have been killed by his wife Queen Eleanor in 1176.

When she was buried legend has it that she held a sprig of heather in her hand – this spectre is dressed in period clothes and also carries a sprig of heather.

Now called the Akeman Inn after the ancient road.

CROSS

Some took their name from the Eleanor Crosses, built by her husband Edward I to commemorate the last journey of Eleanor of Castile. Others have shown the red cross of the Knights Templars; there had been one also called the Red Cross – long before that worldwide organisation was ever thought of – which dispensed clothing to local people. Strangely, I have never seen a cross referring to the Christian faith. Presumably the church would have much to say over such a move.

Great Bromley, Essex. In 2015 this pub was up for sale as a development opportunity. However, the local people were not having their pub turned into a whatever! They bought the Cross and turned it into a community pub, which now offers a post office and a library service. The pub is now called the Great Bromley Cross.

When the government edict closed all pubs due to the coronavirus outbreak they sold their beer as a take-away at £2 a pint. Wonderful!

CROSS KEYS

Cross Keys were a widespread emblem as pub signs. They are a Christian symbol referring to St Peter, as Jesus Christ had said unto him that he would give him the keys of the Kingdom of Heaven. As St Peter was the first Pope, they have been the arms of the Papacy. They survived the reformation and the Puritans because Cross Keys feature in the arms of the Archbishop of York, the Bishop of Gloucester, along with various saints, although when Henry VIII broke with Rome, diplomatically a number of the signs changed to the King's Head.

They were a common sign prior to the Reformation and were usually found in Parish churches dedicated to St Peter.

Later the keys took on a new significance when watchmen kept guard throughout the night on behalf of the community.

Pulloxhill, Bedfordshire. A two-storey building constructed in 1640, it had two gables facing the road with cream-coloured rendering. A central porch entrance completes the picture.

A large six-acre garden with a patio containing tables and chairs is at the rear. This pub must be very unusual as it has been run by the same family for over forty-five years. (I wonder if they have been accepted by the village yet?)

Finally the hanging sign shows a pair of crossed keys with St Peter in the background.

A cavalier who was murdered nearby haunts this pub. He is said to have a neat pointed beard, wears a plumed hat and wears a long. dark cloak. Although he is not alone, another, a Grey Lady, sits by the inglenook fireplace in the bar, and there have been other unexplained occurrences in the pub.

St Albans, Hertfordshire. It was between this inn and the Chequers that Yorkists forced an entry shouting their war cry – 'A-Warwick! A-Warwick!' – in the second battle for the town in February 1461.

Totternhoe, Bedfordshire. The village has been occupied since Roman times, when there was a fort there, as it commands wide views over the surrounding land. It was mentioned in the Domesday Book as *Totene Hou*, meaning look-out house.

A Grade II listed, two-storey thatched and half-timbered building with three dormer windows peeping out from under the thatch.

There is an interior fireplace dated 1433, which is believed to have been built as part of a cottage.

Has been unlucky in respect of fires; the first one was in 1966 while the most recent one was in June 2004; in both cases the thatched roof was destroyed.

A swinging sign shows a pair of crossed keys with St Peter in the background.

White Notley, Essex. During the eighteenth century, a halt for wagoners taking timber from Maldon to Braintree. Any wagoner on his first visit had to pay his 'footing' by buying drinks all round. He completed his initiation by fixing a coin on the wall with a nail specially forged by the village blacksmith. Many of these coins remain beside the front window of the pub.

CROWN

Possibly began life as a sign when an inn was on Crown property, or as a symbol of loyalty to the throne and patriotism.

Amersham, Buckinghamshire. Earliest date recorded was 1620. A coaching inn with eighteenth century front and cobbled courtyard; the interior is Tudor with oak beams, panelling and snug corners – one of the first interiors in Palladium style by Robert Adam.

Petty Sessions were held in the house from the reign of Elizabeth I until 1879. It was customary to display the Arms in rooms where justices sat, be it in inns or elsewhere.

In what is now the lounge is a wall painting of a Tudor coat of arms inscribed "'God bless the Queen'". This has quartering's of England and France, with lion and dragon supporters. A reproduction of the original, seen beside it, was damaged by fire in 1935. Tradition says the painting was done to commemorate a visit of Queen Elizabeth to Shardeloes, a sixteenth century mansion just outside the town, the ancestral home of the Tyrwhitt-Drake family, Lords of the Manor in Amersham.

Bildeston, Suffolk. Built in 1495 by a wool merchant close to the square. It is the oldest inn in the town, retaining inglenook fireplace and ancient beams. The shade of an unknown man in long overcoat and tricorn hat has been seen sitting in a corner of the main bar; a lady in grey looks out of a window, waving to departing guests; two children in Victorian dress appear in different places around the inn; and a cleric has been detected by several visiting mediums.

Strange hammering was thought by the landlord to be boys intent on mischief. He was surprised when, hearing knocking on the front door, he looked out of an upstairs window to see nobody standing there – yet the noise continued. Poltergeist activity has been reported of loud footsteps in upstairs corridors. Guests, on investigating, saw and discovered nothing, but on returning to their room found it incredibly cold. More recently, a relative of a one-time landlord was staring into a mirror upstairs when a strange shape was seen standing behind her which, when she turned, had vanished.

Great Casterton, Leicestershire. Here was a Roman town on the Ermine Street which had a *mansio* or hostelry where official travellers were accommodated and given a change of horses. The present inn is possibly on this ancient site which would have been beside the Roman road gate.

Green End, Bedfordshire. Clothes disappear and reappear somewhere else; footsteps are heard on the stairs and crossing the room. Locals believe this to be Old Pork and Lard, as his ghost appears to have been well fed and watered. His shade is described as a large man wearing a striped waistcoat with leather trousers. He was a former butcher-publican who married a young girl when in his seventies but died just before the birth of his child. Perhaps he cannot rest as he wants to see his child, or 'helps' his wife by putting things away. Supposedly well off, he may return to seek money he had hidden.

Northill, Bedfordshire. The pub has been built on the site of a monastery once owned by the Knights Hospitallers. Monks have been seen walking in the car park as well as climbing stairs in the pub itself.

Old Dalby, Leicestershire. Not on a main highway but standing in a narrow lane and reached via a gated road. This group of red-brick buildings on different levels began as a farmhouse in 1690 and is composed of several tiny rooms. Open fires, traditional furniture and oak beams retain the atmosphere. There are prints on the walls, some of them depicting the Quorn Hunt which meets here. It is also the venue for the National Petanque Championships, a game resembling boules.

Penn, Buckinghamshire. This inn is next to the Holy Trinity Church, where David Blakely is buried. He was shot outside the Magdala pub by his lover Ruth Ellis, who was the last woman to be hanged in the United Kingdom. Although she was buried in a prison grave, she was later reinterred to Amesbury.

The two of them were frequent visitors to the Crown; she now is supposed to haunt it. Hoping for happy times to return, perhaps?

CROWN AND ANCHOR

The badge of the Lord High Admiral, and the arm badge of the Royal Navy's Chief Petty Officers. It was also the name given to a game of dice popular in the trenches during WWI. A piece of cloth would be marked with the four card suites, a crown and an anchor; three dice would be similarly marked then wagers would be made as to which symbols showed face up when the dice were rolled.

Another story tells that if the reigning monarch visited a town, a 'Crown' or the prefix 'Royal' could be added.

It also shows the association between the Navy and Royalty.

Tetney, Lincolnshire. This pub ghost has a grudge against the clock in the bar which it regularly throws about. The clock will suddenly fly from the wall only to land some distance away when no one is near the thing. Dark shadows are also seen, which according to local stories, could be the souls of past smugglers caught in the tunnels under the pub when the tide was flooding.

CROWN HOUSE HOTEL

Great Chesterford, Essex. Constructed in the fifteenth century, it is one of a number of elegant buildings in the area. In the following century it was an inn called the Kings Head; later it was renamed the Crown Inn, then finally the Crown House.

While King Charles II was staying at nearby Audley End it is reputed that Nell Gwyn resided here so they could meet in something like privacy – although heaven only knows why, when most of the country knew of his philandering with her.

The hotel is haunted by half a ghost who is supposed to be a past landlord. The poor chap appears from the only the waist down; he is described as wearing buckled shoes and a blue apron.

CUCKOO BUSH

Gotham, Nottinghamshire. The two-storey red-brick L-shaped building opposite the graveyard was built in 1858 on the site of an earlier one.

The pub name commemorates the legend of the 'Wise Fools of Gotham', who thought that the cuckoo being the harbinger of summer – when all have plenty to eat and the weather is fair – though that if they trapped the cuckoo summer would last the whole year, so they built a fence around the tree where the bird was singing. Sadly for them they forgot to put on a roof, so the bird flew away when it was ready. There are several tales of 'madness' in the village; in one they tried to drown an eel; in another they burned down a forge to get rid of a wasps' nest. One other tale tells how a man rode with a sack of grain on his shoulder so as to ease the burden on his horse. The story's are no doubt kept alive today over a glass or two of beer at the inn.

But there could also be a logical reason for this 'madness'; when at a time it was believed to be contagious. One story tells that King John decided to ride through the village, which did not sit well with the villagers, as any route taken by the King automatically became a public road and the parish would be responsible for its upkeep, so when the King heard of the foolishness he quickly changed his route.

Conversely, another version tells that King John wanted to build a hunting lodge near the village, which would mean even stricter surveillance of the forest and woods than at present; this would make it even harder to poach. So by their antics he was persuaded to go elsewhere.

The village also features in folk tales, and of course the fame of the village has spread to America, where both Washington Irving and Bill Finger named their respective imaginary cities 'Gotham'. Bill Finger, co-creator of *Batman*, had Gotham City peopled by madmen and the like, loosely based on New York Washington Irving's *Salmugundi* is also a parody of New York and its opinions in the nineteenth century; it too was called Gotham.

The swinging sign shows the men of Gotham labouring to build the fence while the cuckoo looks on.

> There is no such thing as a bad pub –
> just that some are better than others.
>
> ***Anon.***

DABBLING DUCK

In centuries past ducks were bred widely in Norfolk before being 'walked' to London markets.

Great Massingham, Norfolk. Was licensed in 1854 as the Rose and Crown, then rebuilt in 1890. When threatened with permanent closure and being converted into housing a forward-thinking local council bought the property then sold it on to two local men on the condition it remained a pub. Reopened in 2006 as 'The Dabbling Duck', the character of the building has been retained.

The name comes from a number of ponds close by in the village where the ducks do indeed dabble.

The swinging sign shows a couple of mallards with one 'dabbling'. Shades of Ducks Ditty from the Kenneth Grahame book *The Wind in the Willows*.

DAIRYMAID

The name of a stagecoach which ran between London and Buckinghamshire, as well as the traditional meaning of a milkmaid.

Aylesbury, Buckinghamshire. The pub was built in the 1960s and is of open plan design with a central bar. The room has two parts; one for sitting and having a chat the other with screens, a pool table, etc. Outside there is a covered smoking area with a screen with a beer garden, some decked seating and a play area for children.

The swinging sign shows a maid pouring milk from a pitcher into a larger bowl.

DASHWOOD ARMS

In 1698 Francis and Samuel Dashwood bought the West Wycombe estate from their brother-in-law Thomas Lewis.

In the 1740s Sir Francis Dashwood had the local villagers excavate the caves in order to find them employment after a number of failed harvests. The chalk removed was then used to construct the road between West and High Wycombe. Later the caves became famous as the venue of the Knights of Sir Francis of Wycombe, better known as the 'Hell Fire Club', whose members featured many of the leading citizens of England and Ireland. Sir Francis Dashwood, 1708-81, Member of Parliament, Chancellor of the Exchequer and later Postmaster General, was a leading light in the promotion of this club.

Sir Edward Dashwood, 12th Baronet, is the Premier Baron of Great Britain.

Piddington, Buckinghamshire. A two-storey painted brick cottage-type pub, with a large single-storey lean-to at one end.

DEEPING STAGE

Market Steeping, Lincolnshire. The building was constructed in 1802 as a coaching inn, first known as the New Inn. It was built so the coaches on the Great North Road as they crossed the bridge over the River Welland would enter directly into the courtyard.

The hotel was renamed in 1975 after a nine-month 'conversion'.

A story has it that in 1846 as a coach was pulling into the stable yard a large hole appeared into which the horses and coach fell. The ghosts of the horses whinnying and the crash of the coach as it fell into the hole can still be heard. Several dead bodies were taken to the inn to await a coroner's verdict. They seem to like it there and stayed – they too haunt the pub. A most unusual happening and haunting.

DICK TURPIN

Tempsford, Bedfordshire. This seventeenth century timber-framed two-storey building with concrete roof tiles stood on the north-bound side of the Great North Road. It is a Grade II listed building, having been refaced with colour-washed brick sometime during the nineteenth century. It had a traditional layout of two bars, with beams and wooden floors. Started life as a beer house in 1846 but are not told what it was beforehand, it only became the Dick Turpin in the twentieth century, possibly when it acquired a full on licence in March 1959.

It has since closed, and the last time I passed by it was a Chinese restaurant.

DINTON HERMIT

Simon Mayne, former owner of Dinton Hall, was among those who passed sentence on Charles I and one of the Puritan signatories on the death warrant. At Charles II's restoration, Mayne was confined to the Tower, where he died in 1661. His servant, John Bigg, 1629-96, was so affected by his master's fate his mental health deteriorated and he spent the rest of his life in a cave, foraging in the countryside as a hermit, thus providing the name of this inn. Another tale tells us that he was one of the executioners. (How many did it take?) He never begged but relied on kindness from the local people and his clothes, long since ragged, were nailed together with bits of leather, the only things he asked for. One of his shoes, made up of several hundred pieces, is in the Ashmolean Museum.

Ford, Buckinghamshire. A sixteenth century beautiful stone, two-storey building with a tiled roof which at one time was a coaching house on the Aylesbury to Thame route.

The pub is now closed. Another unique pub name gone for ever.

DOG AND BADGER

Maulden, Bedfordshire. The first mention of a building on the site was in 1728 when it was a dwelling house; six years later it was a beer house called the Badger. By 1845 when it was sold, it was known as the Dog and Badger.

The present two-storey building, with three dormer windows and steeply pitched roof, suggests that it is not the original cottages.

Inside it has an open-plan bar with the serving counter in one corner, a twin-sided fire set in a bare-brick chimney separates two areas, while there is a couple of small steps leading to a third.

Outside there is a large garden in front of the pub with a children's play area. The swinging sign shows a terrier looking down at a badger.

DOG AND PHEASANT

Mersea Island, Essex. A new pub was built beside the original which had been the village pub since circa 1750.

Mersea, being an island, had only one road in, so along with its proximity to the sea and France the old pub was a haven for smugglers as a meeting place.

A pond close by had a deep well in the middle, where weighted kegs were lowered into until they were wanted or those dastardly Revenue men had gone away.

Documents from 1769 call it the Grey Goose and a tithe map of 1838 also uses that name, but by 1855 the name had changed to the Dog and Partridge.

DURHAM OX

A Durham Ox pub usually takes its name from a castrated bull born in 1796, which was bred by Charles Colling of Ketton Hall, near Darlington, where it was known as the Ketton Ox. It was later sold to John Day of Lincolnshire for £250, who changed the name to The Durham Ox; he exhibited the animal all over England and Scotland, earning him a large amount of money. One day's takings in London was £97. When it died the beast weighted 189 stone (over 2,600lb).

Wellow, Nottinghamshire. Haunted by the shade of a woman who was knocked down by a runaway horse; the body was then taken to the pub to await an inquest. She liked it so much she stayed and still wanders round the building, but is passive. Another phantom is thought to be a former customer who died while having a drink in the bar.

Was the beer awful that night?

DYING GLADIATOR

Brigg, Lincolnshire. The building is eighteenth century with a Greek-style front porch supporting a full-sized gladiator lying on his side with a bleeding wound in his chest. A famous statue in the Vatican with this name was seen by an innkeeper while on holiday which he liked so much he had a copy made. He placed his version prominently then renamed the pub accordingly. We are not told it was called before.

The modern swinging sign is of a gladiator clad in his armour dying in the arena.

There are no strangers in this bar,
only friends who have yet to meet.

Anon.

EEL'S FOOT

There are several pubs of this name, all of which are within the Norfolk Broads area, so as one of the signs I have seen shows a fisherman emptying his eel trap into the bottom of his boat, the name probably commemorates the eel catchers whom I can remember as a child.

It is also possibly a corruption of ales-foot, an alternative name for ground ivy.

Eastbridge, Suffolk. This pub was built in 1642; it is close to Minsmere nature Reserve.

On one wall is a list of the landlords since 1906, although it was licensed well before then. as this smugglers' tale will confirm. In about 1775 a cargo of illicit gin was discovered in a barn at nearby Leiston. The preventative officer in charge looked to a pair of Dragoons billet at the White Horse in Leiston for help, but they were drunk. He sent for two more billeted at the Eel's Foot pub, but before they left the landlady plied them with drink, so by the time they arrived they too were drunk.

When the preventative man arrived at the barn with some men he was delayed by several of the smugglers until their colleagues had emptied the barn. Only then did they open the empty barn; as soon as the revenue men stepped inside the door was shut, locking the men inside while the smugglers made their escape with the booty.

The swinging sign shows an eel with its tail in a boot.

EIGHT BELLS

More usually signifies the peal of eight bells common in many churches but can also refer to the eight bells marking the end of the second dogwatch (6-8-pm) on board ship. A dogwatch lasted two hours, the shortest watches.

Hatfield, Hertfordshire. Seventeenth century. Low-roofed, timber-framed and gabled, it is altered little since it was first built. Another inn with an association with Dick Turpin.

Dickens referred to this inn as having been visited by Bill Sykes in *'Oliver Twist'*.

ELEPHANT AND CASTLE

There are several theories as to the origins of the name. Cutlers were known to have been working in London during the second and third centuries AD; the very word derives from the Latin *cutellarius*, meaning a maker of weapons that have a cutting edge. They continued to make weapons of war until about the end of the sixteenth century, when the need for such weapons decreased; only then did they turn to the domestic market.

On 4th December, 1416, the Worshipful Company of Cutlers' received a royal charter from Henry V in recognition of weapons supplied for Agincourt the previous year; this was an important step forward, as they were now allowed to own property, amongst other privileges. A coat of arms was first granted around 1476 and in 1622 this was modified to its current design which consist of two elephants supporting a shield which has three sets of crossed swords surmounted by an elephant carrying a castle which had two pennants flying.

The motto underneath reads *'Pour Parvenir a Bonne Poy'* ('to succeed through good faith').

The elephants represented the ivory used in the handles of their products and the crossed swords indicated the weapons they used to make.

In 1515 the Worshipful Company of Cutlers was placed eighteenth in the order of the City Companies.

By the middle of the eighteenth century most of the cutlers had moved to

Sheffield, where steel and water for power were freely available; here the office of Master Cutler was second in importance only to the Lord Mayor.

Another explanation of the name relates it is a corruption of 'Infanta of Castile', a piece of foreign language that Londoners in the seventeenth century would be unlikely to even try to get their tongues around, especially as it alluded to a foreigner to whom King Charles I was engaged.

There is a third story; it is said to derive from the skeleton of an elephant dug up near Battle Bridge on London's River Fleet in 1714. Fleet is Anglo-Saxon for 'tidal estuary'; it rises on Hampstead Heath and flows into the Thames, about where Blackfriars Bridge now stands.

There is one other possibility in that the name copies the war elephants that carried a large howdah full of troops or archers.

It was also a trademark adopted by a brewery when it began to send ale to the army in India.

Amersham, Buckinghamshire. The pub is haunted by a lady spook dressed in black who is thought to be responsible for pinching the barmaid's bottoms.

EMBANKMENT

Bedford Town. Built in 1891 in mock-Tudor style with three gable ends facing the road; it is across the road from the River Great Ouse.

Takes the name from its position on the Embankment at Bedford.

The swinging sign shows someone sculling on the river, which is very apt, as the long, straight stretch outside the pub is frequently used for such races.

ENGINEER

Harpenden, Hertfordshire. A two-storey whitewashed brick building. Was originally called the Bird in Hand but changed its name to Engineer in 1868 to commemorate the railway coming to Harpenden and to the men who built the railway.

There is no traditional swinging sign, but two large signs on the front wall of gold lettering on grey green background proclaim the name.

Other signs around the country show Isambard Brunel, and I have seen one showing a Sapper of the Napoleonic Wars.

ENGLISH ROSE

Luton, Bedfordshire. This red-brick building has been a pub since 1845; it was originally called the Rabbit, as that area of the town was called Coney Heath before it became built up.

During the 1919 Peace Day riots by ex-servicemen who were unhappy with their likelihood of employment, this was one of the pubs that the mobs met and no doubt fortified themselves – before marching into town and setting fire to the town hall. Another claim to fame is that the landlord's son courted and married actress Diana Dors.

It is a one bar pub with a rather nice garden/patio which has. apart from the normal wood tables and benches, small, intimate wooden huts with seats and a table. Nice idea!

The swinging sign shows a red rose on a black background.

ESSEX SERPENT

It was a pub frequented by the porters and others who used the market a few yards away. One customer in his nineties remembered being taken to the pub when he was a lad, as his dad worked as a fruit and vegetable market porter. A full waiter service was on the first-floor restaurant for those who wanted it, while the public bar on the ground floor would have catered for thirsty workers.

The pub sign was said to derive from the armorial bearings of Robert Devereux, Earl of Essex, who was executed for treason at the Tower of London on February 25th, 1601, having led a failed revolt against Elizabeth I.

An alternative is proffered in a book called *The History of Sign Boards*; Jacob Larwood suggests that this sign is an allusion to a fabulous monster recorded in a broadside of 1704, from which we learn that before Henry II died a dragon of marvellous bigness was discovered at St Osyth, in Essex. Legend has it that a dragon had a lair in the cellars of the Priory at St Osyth.

> Survival of the fittest: with the Scots it was whisky or perish –
> My! How they have survived!
>
> *Anon.*

FALCON

There are a number of meanings for the word falcon; the first is the common name given to bird of prey which were used for falconry.

It was a Yorkist sign during the Civil War.

A sign in Stratford on Avon shows Shakespeare's crest; a falcon supporting a spear above the motto '*non sans droict*' ('not without right'). Finally it could be a small piece of field artillery with a bore of two-and-a-half inches which could fire a one pound ball almost a mile.

Bletsoe, Bedfordshire. Situated on the banks of the River Ouse west the village, it was once a mill belonging to the St John family until at least 1650. The family who were also Earls of Bolingbroke and lived at Melchbourne Park; many of the family are buried in Bletsoe graveyard.

During 1727 the Bedford to Higham Ferrers road became a turnpike which would increase the traffic considerably, and it is possible that around then the mill building, or part of it, was converted into a coaching house. Certainly the Falcon was there thirty years later, when Lieutenancy meetings were held at the inn.

This L-shaped building has oak beams, open fires with an inglenook, a splendid oak-panelled room, which is now the restaurant, and reputedly a secret tunnel to Bletsoe Castle. A former sign I remember during the 1950s and '60s in the car park asked patrons to 'Please park prettily'

It was the one-time favourite haunt of William Thackeray, and it was here in 1859 that Edward Fitzgerald translated the *'Rubaiyat'*, later describing the inn with the most glowing of terms.

The pub has its own ghost or two; one has the habit of tidying up, whilst another throws bottles and glasses at the staff. The bottle store was part of the old stable which is where, in the 1700's, an ostler died after falling from the hay loft – it is his ghost who is suspected of the mischief, as kitchen staff tell of food going missing when he is about and also report the feeling of being watched.

FEATHERS INN

Usually refers to the emblem of the Prince of Wales which show the three on his crest with the words *'Ich Dien'* ('I Serve') on the ribbon below them.

The first person to adopt three ostrich feathers seems to have been Edward the Black Prince; on his sable shield used for jousting there were three argent.

One theory has it that Edward took both the plume and the motto from blind John of Bohemia after he was killed at the Battle of Crecy in 1346, but little credence is given to the theory as John bore a crest of vultures' wings. Another tells that the motto comes from the Welsh *'Eich Dyn'*. meaning 'behold your man', which was a homophone for *'Ich Dien'* and may have endeared him to the Welsh archers who fought at Crecy.

Wadesmill, Hertfordshire. A two-storey brick building with a portico supported by columns as an entrance.

Once called the Princes Arms but changed the name in 1670. Was one of the busiest coaching inns on the road from London to Cambridge.

At a time when coaches were in and out of the yard, one knocked down and killed a young girl with fair hair. She now haunts the pub and is always crying.

The swinging sign shows the Prince of Wales's feathers on a light blue background. There is also a large board over the door proclaiming the name.

FERRY BOAT INN

North Fambridge, Essex. A five hundred-year-old pub whose foundations are reputedly a bed of reeds. This permits the old plaster and timber-work to move at the dictates of the weather, which doubtless accords for its long life.

Advertised as established in 1591. Wonder how many pubs built today will be still standing in 2500?

FESTIVAL HOUSE

Norwich, Norfolk. A Grade II listed building which started life in the 1800s as a grocery store. It was first licensed in 1898, when the one from the 'Edinburgh' public house was transferred and the 'Cork Cutters Arms' licence surrendered. It took the name of 'Festival House' from the Norfolk and Norwich Triennial Music Festival, which had been held in St Andrews Hall from 1824. It retained the name for almost a century, but of late it has changed hands – and names – a number of times, firstly in 1992 to the Grocers Ghost, in 1993 to Franco's, then back to the Festival House; in 2001 it became an Irish bar called Delaney's.

FIGHTING COCK(S)

The sign usually show a fighting bird which originally indicated that cockfighting was held either on the premises or nearby. An unlikely possibility could also refer to number 43 squadron of the RAF, who were nicknamed the Fighting Cocks, a name which was adopted in 1926 when the squadron was equipped with Gloucester Gamecock aircraft.

When Themistocles was leading his army against the Persians he saw two cocks fighting. Using this as opportunity to boost his forces morale, he told them; the birds were not fighting for their country or their religion or for glory; their only motive was that neither would yield to the other. This speech made such an impression on his troops' fervour they fought and won the battle. After the war the Athenians decreed that one day every year should be set aside for cock-fighting to celebrate the victory.

St Albans, Hertfordshire. An eleventh century building on an eighth century site, which originally may have been a hospice run by monks for travellers and pilgrims who visited the cathedral. The pub is haunted by three monks who are only visible from the knees up; they emerge from the cellar, glide across the bar before sitting at a table by the fire, where they remain for several minutes before disappearing.

FIVE BELLS

In earlier times, sailors could not afford a timepiece of their own, so a system of bells was instigated using at first a timer which measured thirty minutes. Sailors would know if it were morning, afternoon or night, by the number of times the ships bell was rung which would also indicate the time of that shift. The bell was rung every half an hour, so one bell was rung at the end of the first half an hour, two bells at the hour, until eight bells, which was the end of a shift. When five bells were rung sailors would know they were well past the halfway time of a shift.

Burwell, Cambridgeshire. An eighteenth century Grade II listed building. Despite the explanation above, the pub takes its name from the number of bells the local church has, with the swinging sign showing the five.

Cople, Bedfordshire. A seventeenth century building. The swinging sign shows five bells; the name was taken from the church opposite, which at one time had only five bells. Although it now has six, the pub retained its old name.

There is also a nautical connection; the pub is haunted by a sailor who has his hair in a pigtail and sits by the fireplace smoking a pipe.

FLAG

Watford, Hertfordshire. A very large three-storey Victorian building, with stables attached, which is built of khaki brick and stone, with the main entrance having a portico supported by columns. The building was originally the Clarendon Hotel, constructed to attract customers from the nearby railway. Later it was turned into offices for the brewery owners, who at the same time converted the attached stables into a pub which they called the Pennant after the brewery logo; later it became the Flag; then the Flag and Firkin, and finally back to the Flag.

The cavernous bar has wood floors and plenty of mahogany around the bar, and there is large games room. Outside, at the front there are tables and chairs on the pavement, while at the rear there are two large beer gardens.

The swinging sign is the name printed over a black and white Union flag.

FLINTKNAPPERS ARMS

A flintknapper is one who forms flint into useful shapes. It is very apt that the only pub of this name I can find is in Brandon, close to Grimes Graves. These are forty-foot pits and tunnels carved out in Neolithic times to quarry the flints for axe, arrow and spear heads. Although now no longer mined, up until recently Brandon was famous for making gun flints for muzzle-loading guns.

Brandon, Norfolk. A pub built in the Tudor style typical of East Anglia, part-timbered with herringbone brick infill and leaded windows. The modern swinging sign does not show a picture of an old knapper at work, as I remember, but three of what seems to be spear heads.

FLITCH OF BACON

Little Dunmow, Essex. Seventeenth century or earlier Grade II listed building. A board on the first floor of the inn sign tells;

> Painted in gold ye flitch behold Of famed Dunmow ye boaste
> Then should there call fond couples all And pledge it in a toaste.

This commemorates the Dunmow Flitch, a side of cured pork, awarded since AD 1104 to any couple able to prove to a jury 'not to have quarrelled nor repented of their marriage within one year and one day after the celebration'.

Couples winning the flitch could make money by selling slices to bystanders. It was even mentioned in Chaucer's 'Canterbury Tales' by the Wife of Bath.

In the eighteenth century it seemed the award waned somewhat, but the custom was revived after the publishing of a book by William Harrison Ainsworth titled 'The Customs of Dunmow', which seemed to have caught the interest of Victorians. Nowadays it is only awarded on Whit Monday during a leap year.

The hanging sign is a three-dimensional side of bacon. It is, of course, a unique pub name.

FLYING BEDSTEAD

Hucknall, Nottinghamshire. Being named in commemoration of an experimental aircraft developed at the nearby Hucknall aerodrome in the 1950s which looked like a bedstead and which went on to be developed into the Harrier Jump Jet.

The pub was a modern 1950/60 design but has now been closed and is awaiting demolition. The swinging sign showing the 'Flying Bedstead' has been saved and is now on the wall of a 'Micro Pub' nearby.

At least the sign has been saved, even if the pub has gone. Perhaps one day someone will open another pub of this unique name.

FOUR BELLS

Woodborough, Nottinghamshire. This has been a pub since 1762 and has had more names than enough, having been called at different times 'The Bell', 'Bell', 'Ring 'o' Bells', 'Five Bells' and 'Eight Bells'. You must admit, all the names do have a similar ring to them.

A two-storey half-timbered building in the late Tudor style with herringbone brick infill and small leaded lights which carry the name of the pub. The swinging sign shows four gold bells on a black background.

FOUR HORSESHOES

Thornham Magna, Suffolk. Dating from circa 1150 – which makes it the oldest pub in Suffolk.

The pub, as befits its age, is haunted by an old woman and her daughter. Although there is no tangible story behind the manifestations, it is thought they perished in a fire at some time. To reinforce this theory, residents have been woken in the night by a noise and an overpowering sensation of heat. It also has a mischievous poltergeist who switches electrical appliances on when a room is empty.

The swinging sign shows four gold horseshoes on a drab bottle-green background.

FOUR SWANS

Waltham Cross, Hertfordshire. The Four Swans claims to have been built circa 1260, as proclaimed on its gantry sign, which stretched across the road, supporting four carved swans. Waltham Cross was the last but one resting place for the bier containing Queen Eleanor's body in 1290. So it is reasonable to assume there must have been some sort of accommodation in the village, probably at the inn, especially as it was on a main road connecting London with Cambridge, Ely and King's Lynn. The pub was rebuilt in the seventeenth century, where it continued to service the traveller for the next one hundred years, or until the railway put paid to the trade.

Sadly the building was demolished in the 1960s to make way for a multi-storey garage – not a fair exchange, I think!

However, the gantry, along with the swans, still stands over the high street in the town, so not all has been lost.

FOX

A natural predator in the countryside and now scavenger in the towns. In days gone by every countryman would recognise one, so it was a good name for a pub. Alternately, in some coastal areas, a fox was a piece of twisted rope as used on boats.

There is also a family line of eighteenth century landowners called Fox. A rhyme that often accompanied the sign was;

I am a fox you plainly see,
There is no harm can come to me,
My master has placed me here,
To let you know he sells good beer.

Hallaton, Leicestershire. A Hare Pie Scramble and Bottle Kicking are held every Easter Monday in the town, a tradition which dates back to at least the late eighteenth century and maybe based on a pagan rite. A brass band heads a procession from the inn to the rectory, where a large square pie of hare is collected and cut up. Some of it is put in a sack and the remainder distributed to the crowd. Returning with the sack to the inn, three bottles (actually beer kegs) are collected and carried to the Hare Pie Bank, where the sack is emptied and the pieces snatched as trophies. There is then a 'bottle kicking' contest between villagers of Hallaton and Medbourne, the object being to kick the bottle over their own brook in a contest of the best of three. The winners are presented with the beer in the kegs, by which time it surely tastes terrible. After a token sample, the rest of the festivities are spent in the Fox Inn, though other sources say this honour is shared also with the Royal Oak (now closed) and the Bewicke Arms in Hallaton.

The pub has an appropriately named Hare Pie restaurant.

FOX AND FIDDLER

Colchester, Essex. Built in 1420, although other parts are sixteenth century Tudor but greatly altered over the years.

During its life the pub has been known as the Ship, the Headgate, Elephant and Castle, and Boudicca. It is haunted by a chambermaid called Sarah from the 1640s, who was found hiding in the cellar with other women by that dreadful person, the Witchfinder General, Matthew Hopkins. She was accused of witchcraft and was reputedly chained to a wall in the cellar then bricked up to die. She is regularly sighted, being described as having long blonde hair, wearing a lace cap and white pinafore over a black dress.

The origins of this unusual pub name is somewhat obscure; the only information I could find out was that a former landlord had altered it when he took over. The swinging sign shows a fox laying on the moon with a fiddler silhouetted against it – a parody on the nursery rhyme, perhaps?

FOX AND HOUNDS

Barley, Hertfordshire. A pub since 1797; before that it was a hunting lodge used by James I when in the Royston area. A building on several levels, it has one very large chimney. Inside are many small rooms with log fires placed either side of this massive centrally placed chimney, with benefit to all.

A fine, and now rare, gallows sign extends across the road and carved on it in silhouette is a fox with huntsmen and hounds in full cry. It commemorates a famous chase when the hard-pressed fox was eventually run to earth in the yard of the inn.

The swinging sign is a comic one, with Mr Fox sitting down for a meal with a couple of hounds.

Now closed and may have been turned into housing.

A cask of wine works more miracles than a church full of saints.

English proverb.

GALLON POT

Great Yarmouth, Norfolk. The initial building on this site was constructed in 1772 by William Burroughs as a wine lodge; it was then bought by a local brewery in 1897. The original was destroyed by bombs during WWII. The present pub was built in 1959 by the brewer owner.

The swinging sign shows an ancient gentleman holding his gallon tankard, and on the corner is a pillar with a three-dimensional overlarge gallon pot.

GARDENERS ARMS

Norwich, Norfolk. The building dates back to 1530, although another source says 1696. The pub has a grisly nickname of the Murders.

In 1895 the landlord's daughter, Millie, moved back in the pub, away from her estranged husband, Frank Miles. The day before the murder they had rowed; he returned the following day and murdered Millie with a 'bung picker' (a tool used in the brewery where he worked). He immediately gave himself up at a police station and was committed for trial on a charge of murder. Sentenced to hang, the case caused a public outcry as there was some doubt regarding Millie's promiscuity. So the sentence was commuted to life imprisonment. Frank Miles served ten years before applying for parole – he died of a heart attack while the case was being heard.

The hanging sign is a shield featuring a man tending plants; surmounting the shield is a knight's helmet, above which is a basket of grapes. To one side stands a woman with an armful of produce.

GEORGE

There are a number of choices here, from the Hanoverian Kings to the name of a ship or England's patron saint. Of the Kings, George III and IV seem to be the most popular, possibly because there was a great deal of building going on at the time as the 'Industrial Revolution' was in full swing.

Doddington, Cambridgeshire. One of the strangest and as yet unexplained haunting in the pub world. Just before opening for business a crowd of people can be heard waiting outside, obviously wanting a drink. However, when the doors are opened, the noise stops and there is no one in sight!

Huntingdon, Cambridgeshire. A coaching inn, records of which date back to Henry VIII. Sold in 1550 to Henry Cromwell, who had attended the grammar school opposite. He was grandfather to Oliver, who, so it is said locally, was born at the inn.

Charles I used the hotel as his headquarters in 1645 during the English Civil War, probably prior to the battle of Naseby.

Two sides remain of a seventeenth century courtyard, one of which has an open gallery and outside staircase. The rooms opening on to it are also seventeenth century, with timbered ceilings. One of them with a clear view of the entrance is said to have been Dick Turpin's room when he used this road. It had a tiny closet with a spy-hole which is now sealed. The front was destroyed by fire and rebuilt in the nineteenth century style.

Shakespeare's plays have been produced annually in the courtyard during the last week of June and first of July since 1959.

Luton, Bedfordshire. A three-storey red-brick building with a slate roof; originally it appears to have been two buildings, so some time in the past its neighbour was converted into an extra bar. Built circa 1870, it is a Grade II listed building.

The pub has unusual hooped shop windows on the ground floor.

Named after George II which is unusual for a pub, especially as he had been dead for over a hundred years. George II was the last English king to lead his troops into battle, which was at Dettingen during 1743.

The pub has a resident ghost; the man was killed when working on the nearby railway sometime in the early 1900. His body was taken to the pub to await the police and to arrange an inquest. He liked it so much he stayed; fortunately he appears to be benign, just showing his face occasionally.

Silsoe, Bedfordshire. The original George Hotel was in existence during 1613, when it was conveyed to Richard Daniel for the princely sum of 240 pounds 10 shillings and sixpence, which included eleven acres of ground dispersed round the village. Even with the land the price was quite high, which may indicate that the George was already well established. The George then would have been Saint George.

John Byng, 5th Viscount Torrington, visited the hotel a number of times, recording in his diary not only his thoughts of the place but prices too.

In 1838 the licence was removed to a new building nearby as the old one was 'untenantable and irreparable'.

The new hotel is a beautiful Georgian building, built probably circa 1838, originally as a coaching inn, when the village was a staging post between Bedford and Luton.

The sign shows a painting of King George IV which could date it accurately.

In the eighteenth century Lady Elizabeth Grey – a member of the de Grey family, who were the Earls of Kent – fell in love with a coachman who worked at the inn. As her father objected to such a tryst she hid out at the inn for several weeks; however, her father found out where she was hiding and went to fetch her home.

The couple tried to escape in a carriage, but it crashed into a nearby lake, drowning them both. She had now taken up residence as the pub ghost but appears to be quite benign.

The pub was closed the last time I passed in 2015, although it looked like an Indian restaurant.

Update; the village is trying to buy the building to retain it as a community hub.

GEORGE AND DRAGON

Saint George was thought to be a soldier of Cappadocian Greek origins, a member of the Praetorian Guard for the Roman emperor Diocletian. He was sentenced to death for refusing to recant his Christian belief. He was canonised in AD 494 by Pope Gelasius.

St George is the patron saint of a number of things and countries beside England. The dragon is a symbol of the evil and is only a visual allegory, the same as St Michael conquering Satan or Perseus's rescue of Andromeda or any other on the many folk stories which abound in the world.

There is an ancient rhyme under some signs which add a touch of humour;

> To save a mayd St George the Dragon slew,
> A pretty tale if all is told be true,
> Most say there are no dragons, and it's sayd
> There was no George; pray God there was a mayd.

According to the Golden Legend, St George slew the dragon in a place called Silene in Libya, that country being exotic enough to have dragons. It tells the town had a dragon living in a small lake, and to appease the dragon they fed it two sheep a day, but when they ran out of sheep they were forced to feed it their own children, selected by lottery. One day the King's daughter was chosen, and despite offering all his wealth no one would take her place. The daughter was duly sent to the lake clothed in a wedding dress. Fortunately our hero chose that time and day to pass by, then, seeing the dragon emerge from the lake, he charged it and with his lance wounded the beast. He called to the princess to throw him her girdle, which he placed round the dragon's neck when it became meek.

In the town George offered to kill the dragon if they all became Christians and were baptised. The King was so grateful he built a church on the site, where the dragon had been killed. Traditionally the sword used by St George was called Ascalon. There are later versions of the myth, but only the details differ.

This story was probably bought back by the men from the Crusades.

On establishment of the Order of the Garter by Edward III in 1348, St George was adopted as the patron of the order.

After the civil war when Puritans ruled, they ordered that only saints specifically mentioned in the Bible should be venerated. Luckily for England, most people either ignored the decree or adapted the story to suit the situation.

Prior to the Hanoverian Georges, pubs called by the name George, almost certainly referred St George.

West Wycombe, Buckinghamshire. This is one of the three inns that survive from nine existed during the great coaching days. Built about 1720, it replaces an older inn, reputedly fourteenth century. Originally of brick but now refaced with stucco. The heavy oval sign made of lead showing George slaying the dragon may be as old as the inn and is considered one of the most unusual in the country.

The arch leading to the yard where stagecoaches used to pull up remains, as does the mounting stone for horsemen.

The inn has a trio of ghosts. Footsteps heard descending the old staircase night after night are reputedly those of a man murdered in one of the rooms. A lady guest, a spiritualist, spoke of psychic phenomena all about her, and of a terrible quarrel on these stairs. When she visited the priest's hole in the inn, which dated from the time of the older building, she was aware of children, but there is no history of haunting by them.

A poltergeist has also been reported, not one that smashes things but one that makes them disappear, though these always turn up again, and staff have come to accept this as just part of the working day.

The coach yard opens into a garden, where, according to legend, the White Lady haunts on dark nights. Sukie, or Susan, a young serving girl employed at the inn about two hundred years ago, was pretty, with long golden hair, it amused her to play suitors off one against the other. The arrival of a young, fashionable and obviously well-off visitor caught her eye, he soon became a regular visitor, something noticed by her young men friends.

The story is one sent her a letter supposedly from this new friend, asking her to meet him in the West Wycombe Caves dressed in a bridal gown, which she anticipated as a proposal. This she did, only to be met and jeered at by her three ex-suitors. Horseplay followed, and she fell, hitting her head. Thinking her merely dazed, the lads carried her back to the George and Dragon. As there was a secret passage from the caves to the inn, put there by Sir Francis Dashwood, owner of the Wycombe Estate, they managed to enter her room and leave her there. When found in the morning, she was dead. Soon after, stories began to circulate of her being seen in the inn and the garden wearing the wedding dress.

GEORGE IV

Often shows the portrait of him sitting on a sofa with his arm extended along the back of it from a portrait by Sir Thomas Lawrence. He is rarely depicted on inn signs, as he was not the most popular of monarchs and only reigned for ten years. He was born at St James's Palace in 1762 and was crowned at Westminster on 19th July, 1821, which at the time caused something of an outrage, as he would not allow his Queen Caroline into the service.

Baldock, Hertfordshire. First recorded as a pub in 1882. It is a two-storey rendered building with a long, covered porch at the front. Outside there is a beer garden with a children's play area.

The swinging sign shows a rather slim and handsome George IV before he became obese.

GOAT INN

Unusual name for a pub. It could come from the word scapegoat, which, in primitive days, had a dogma that said a goat could absorb all the ills and woes of people and animals. It was quite common for a goat or two to be included with a herd of cattle in the belief that the goat would keep the cattle healthy. Another use of this theory was that a goat was paraded round a sick person's house in the hope the disease would be absorbed into the goat's body.

St Albans, Hertfordshire. A fifteenth century two-storey coaching inn; with part of the first floor jettied. The building was originally constructed as a private house but was converted to service the stagecoaches using the A5 in and out of London. It is a Grade II listed building in a terrace of similar houses.

The hanging sign is oval with a painted goat's head with lettering above.

Strange happenings occur in this pub, although no one has seen any of the noisy participants of the rowdy party that happens late at night, which seems to be mainly young ladies who do the carousing, which, as the pub used to be a brothel as well as a coaching house, is more than possible. Another, is the sound of a coach and horses being driven through the arch into what was the pub courtyard.

GOLDEN PHEASANT

Biggleswade, Bedfordshire. An eighteenth century Grade II listed, two-storey building with dormers in the roof and a single bay window on the ground floor. It is a small, whitewashed building in the centre of the town, which became a beer house in 1851 but did not gain a full licence until 1955.

The swinging sign is round, showing a gold glass of beer with hops and barley along with the name round the outside.

The pub is haunted by a singing ghost who performs in an empty bar, and someone else who clumps about in an empty room.

The Golden, or Rainbow pheasant, originates in western China, although there are several flocks of feral birds in the country. Probably descendants of those imported to brighten up large estates in earlier times.

Although an unusual name, there are several others of the ilk.

GREAT WHITE HORSE

Ipswich, Suffolk. Old English name of Gippesiwic or Gippeswyke from the River Gipping, the upper reaches of the Orwell, hence the old name, meaning 'town on the Gipping'.

The Great White Horse is one of the most famous English coaching houses, dating from 1518. Its list of patrons include royalty and the famous. Elizabeth I, visited, then George II, Louis XVIII of France, Lord Nelson and his bit of stuff, the Duke of Windsor after the abdication, to name but a few.

Patronised by Dickens and described by him as an 'overgrown tavern', it was here he set the incident of Mr Pickwick's having lost himself in the many corridors and his encounter with the lady in the yellow curl papers, which is commemorated in murals in the dining room. There was also a Pickwick Room with a four-poster.

Building of this age invariably have ghosts; the White Horse is no exception. It has a number. One is unusual, to say the least; a pair of leather boots marching, but without any feet in them! Another speaks only French, while the Grey Lady makes an occasional appearance. A further apparition is a little girl called Flossie Floyd, who was burnt to death in a fire during the 1920s, so the building is not completely empty.

Closed circa 2007, it is now several retail outlets. Despite the ravishes of the twenty-first century, after five centuries the Great White Horse can still hold its head up high with the hope someone will rescue it.

GREENGAGE

The greengage is a small green or greenish yellow plum first bred in Moissac, France, from a green fruited wild plum found in Asia Minor – the original cultivar survives almost unchanged as 'Reine Claude Verte'.

The plum was introduced into England from France in 724 by Sir William Gage (1657-1727), an English botanist. His home, Hengrave Hall, near Bury St Edmunds, was built between 1525-38, largely of stone from nearby Ixworth Priory, which was dissolved in 1536, and white bricks made at Woolpit.

The building was used as a convent until 1974, then as the Hengrave Community until 2005. At present it is used for wedding receptions and other functions.

Bury St Edmunds, Suffolk. Built in 1957, the licence was transferred from the George when it closed. The pub has three bars which include a traditional public one.

GREEN MAN

The Green Man is a mysterious figure that transcends religion and cultures; it has had any number of transformations in different beliefs, although still remaining basically what we see today.

Generally a Green Man is a representation of a face surrounded by, or made up of, branches and foliage, sometimes used as an architectural ornament. The face appeared on temple friezes throughout the Roman Empire, from which it may have been adapted. He appears in almost every country in Europe, and many similar images appear on Asian, Indian and Arabian architecture, some of which date back three thousand years or more. An early Christian example appears on the tomb of St Abre in St Hillaire-le-Grand, dated around AD 400, although it did not appear in Christian England until later.

Some believe him to be the keeper of the forest, others believe he represents an ancient vegetation deity, yet more suggest he is the deity of rebirth and spring, especially those heads with vegetation spewing from their mouths, some of which may contain flowers.

The face may also have developed from older pre-Roman deities such as the Greek Pan or the Gaulish Celtic Cernunnos, which in turn comes from the Celtic 'Derg Corra'. the man in the tree, a trickster who is always accompanied by a trout, a raven and a stag. One of the earliest examples of this figure was discovered on an Irish obelisk dated third century BC.

During the Reformation when pagan imagery was stamped on, the Green

Man were replaced by signs of axe-carrying woodsman or others such as Robin Hood.

In medieval times those who let off fireworks were also called Green Men, due to their wearing foliage round their heads and face; not because they were dressed for some particular celebration. It was for no other reason that the foliage kept the sparks from their faces!

Epping, Hertfordshire. In 1738, Dick Turpin and Tom King were drinking at this inn when the landlord recognised King and grabbed him from behind. Turpin drew his gun, and in the scuffle King was accidentally shot. The same tale is reported as having happened at the Red Lion in Whitechapel. After this Turpin went to Yorkshire taking the name John Palmer, where he became a horse trader but was arrested there after an altercation with a landlord.

GREGORY ARMS

The old manor house was purchased in around 1475 by the De Ligne family, who occupied it. The building stood empty from about 1789 until 1857, when it was demolished; in the meantime the present Harlaxton Manor had been built.

The family tree for the De Ligne's like many other old families, is far too complicated to explain. Suffice to say, George de Ligne inherited a fortune and was responsible for rebuilding much of the village.

Harlaxton, Lincolnshire. Built in 1797 by George de Ligne Gregory, as, when he was passing the Golden Lion after church one Sunday, he was dismayed to find locals sitting outside the pub drinking beer. So he built a new pub on the present site, naming it after the family then closed the one in the centre of the village. However, he only allowed the landlord of the new pub a six-day licence. Aware that they would lose money by this deed, he gave him the sole rights to sell coal in the village to offset the loss. I wonder if that concession is still in force?

Interestingly, it has a number of windows bricked up, probably due to the window tax, which was not repealed until 1851.

After a refurbishment in 2007 the Arms was dropped, so the name is now just The Gregory.

GRIFFIN

Also: griffo, gryphon, griffen. A mythological creature, usually depicted with the body, tail and back legs of a lion, with the head and wings of an eagle, and talons on its front feet. As the lion was considered king of the beasts and the eagle king of the birds, a griffin was thought to be king of all creatures and a symbol of divine power.

Griffins in Greek mythology were considered 'the sharp-toothed hounds of Zeus that have no bark'. They were thought to live in the northern extremes of the world, where they guarded hordes of gold from their greedy neighbours.

Because of its mythological might, it became a symbol of royalty and strength, and was adopted into heraldry, not just in England but throughout the world.

Often seen carved on churches, it is a symbol of Jesus, who was both human and divine, paralleling a griffin, which is a creature of the sky and of the earth.

Waltham Cross, Hertfordshire. There was a pub in Waltham Cross that at one time was frequented by Bedlamites. From this inn a forged Bedlam licence could be obtained for half a crown; apparently, it did a roaring trade. A Bedlamite was a person having served time in the Bedlam hospital, who, on discharge, was given a metal arm badge which would protect them from prosecution for begging, which allowed the holder to follow a lucrative form of vagrancy by levying charity on the plea of insanity.

These real or assumed one-time inmates could beg an easy living playing the fool at fairs or appearing deranged at a cottage or farmhouse.

These figures survived in some parts until the eighteenth century.

GUINEA

The coin was the first machine-struck English coin, which was approximately one quarter ounce of gold; it was originally worth one pound sterling, but the increase in the price of gold meant its value increased up to thirty shilling at one time. To prevent clipping or filing, the edges were milled, as in previous times solid silver coins were regularly 'clipped or filed'. The small amount removed from each coin would add up to a considerable amount over time but also reduce the value of the coinage.

The value was set at twenty-one shillings in 1816. It took its name from the Guinea area of Africa, where much of the gold used to make the coins originated. It was first struck in 1663 and last struck in 1814.

It was customary for professional fees, subscriptions, the price of racehorses and other luxuries to be quoted in guineas up until decimalisation. When it was no longer legal tender. Quite right too, as one pound and five pence didn't quite have the same ring!

Moggerhanger, Bedfordshire. An eighteenth century two-storey brick building with a tiled roof, probably built before 1728. In 1784 a public house in Moggerhanger was auctioned, although it was not named as the Guinea. During the early twentieth century the name was changed to The Old Guinea, not reverting to its original name until 1962.

The swinging sign shows the obverse of a golden guinea, which has King Charles II's head on it with the legend '*Carolvs II dei Gratia*' ('Charles II by the grace of God').

Many a landlord's observation;
I am pleased to see all who pass through these doors –
some on the way in and some on the way out.

HAPPY WANDERER

High Wycombe, Buckinghamshire. Built in the mid-twentieth century and named after the local football team, the first landlord being an ex-member of that team.

Now closed but may have been taken over by an Islamic Society.

HARE AND HOUNDS

A sign all country folk would understand.

Old Warden, Bedfordshire. The first reference to the building as a pub was in 1792 when it was called the Crown, a name it retained until circa 1822, after which it was called the Hare and Hounds. When the estate was sold in 1872 to Joseph Shuttleworth the rent for the pub was £25 per annum with £4 7s 6d for the field at the rear. How times have changed!

A long two-storey rendered building painted off-white with a tiled roof. The roof over the first-floor windows is raised in a semi-circle, giving it an almost surprised look of raised eyebrows.

Inside, the rooms stretch the length of the building, with the serving bar splitting the room. A separate dining room is adjacent to the rear of the main one and accessed up two steps. Behind the bar-room is a further private dining room with a beautiful table that seats twelve.

Decoration is a number of photographs of the aircraft displayed at the nearby Shuttleworth collection, along with some of local interest.

Access to the toilets is slightly restricted for the disabled as it means navigating a step, although grab handles are in place.

The pub is reputedly haunted by ghostly woman who disappears into thin air after a few moments.

The pub and village are part of the Shuttleworth Estate, which has a collection of classic cars and aircraft housed on the nearby airfield. Opposite the entrance to the airfield there are the Swiss Garden, also belonging to the estate, which were built by Lord Ongley in the early nineteenth century.

The swinging sign shows a hare sitting watching the hounds milling about in the distance.

St Albans, Hertfordshire. A two-storey timber-framed pub with plastered exterior and a tiled roof, circa 1650. It is a Grade II listed building.

One source tells that it was originally called the Hogshead Ale House; another says it was called the Falcon but changed its name to Hare and Hounds in 1774.

The real story of the pub is about the hangman's tree which used to stand next to it where many a convicted felon met his end. In those days Christian burial for criminals or murderers were not always observed; in this case the bodies were thrown into a pit adjacent to the old pub building which now forms part of the present cellar.

In 1990 a barmaid was going down the steps into the cellar when she saw a black shadows rush past her and an eerie voice shout, "'Get out'". Locals reckoned the grave had opened up and those buried there were escaping.

The swinging sign is a contemporary design that has a white silhouette of a hare and two of hounds.

HARRINGTON ARMS

The Earl of Harrington was created in 1742 by King George II for William Stanhope. They were a local family whose seat was at Eveston Castle.

Long Eaton, Nottinghamshire. In 1759 the road between Lenton and Sawley became a turnpike. Although a charge was made, the improved road surface increased the traffic along that stretch, which made the Harrington quite busy. The building is half three-storey, the other part, two, both have been rendered with a restaurant extension added at one end. This has been constructed to include traditional beams and a local map of the River Trent, with its tributaries and canals, painted on the end wall.

Close to the River Trent, hence the map in the restaurant. The swinging sign shows the coat of arms of the family.

HAYCOCK

Wansford, Cambridgeshire. An inn called the Swan has been on this site for many years, although the exact dates are uncertain; however, there is a stone in the garden dating the present construction to 1632. It was originally a coaching house on the Great North Road between Peterborough and Stamford.

The pub name comes from a folk tale, originally written in Latin by Richard Braithwaite, telling of the adventures had by Drunken Barnaby on his four journeys to the north of England.

On this occasion he fell asleep on a haycock, only to be awakened some time later by shouts; he was astonished to find he was floating on the River Nene, which at the time was given to sudden flooding. Thinking he had floated far out to sea and may be in a foreign land, he called out to watchers asking where he was, and when told 'Wansford. "What!" he cried. "Wansford in England?"

'Wansford in England' is a label which has stuck to the village to this day and appears on the sign.

The building has its ghost, reputedly that of Richard Braithwaite, who stayed at the inn when a Royalist officer during the English Civil War.

Royalty has stayed there; Queen Victoria spent a night there and the unfortunate Mary Queen of Scots also spent a night there on her way to imprisonment at Fotheringhay Castle. Celia Fiennes on her journey through England also stayed there and commented on the folk tale.

The hotel sign is of a man floating on a haycock down the river towards the bridge.

HEATH INN

Heath and Reach, Bedfordshire. Originally The Cock beer house, then The Cock Horse public house and then the Cock Hotel. First licensed in 1838, although that may have been when it changed to a public house.

The pub was not granted a full licence until post-WWII, the name Heath Inn was adopted in 2012 despite the building being in Reach!

The swinging sign is plain with white on a back background.

HERCULES INN

A reference to the strongman of Greek mythology. The greatest of all the Greek heroes; a man of superhuman courage, prowess and fortitude. In Greek mythology he was known as Heracles; in Roman mythology he became Hercules, although most of the stories are the same.

Often shown wearing a lion's skin, which legend has he killed with his bare hands.

Sutton Cheney, Leicestershire. An old coaching inn, parts of which date from the seventeenth century. The ghost in this pub is of Mary McDonagh, who had both hands chopped off for stealing from the pub. When she manifests, which is usually in the dining room, she is wearing a mobcap and black dress.

The pub is opposite the Parish Church where, legend has, Richard III made his last confession before the Battle of Bosworth Field.

HERMIT OF REDCOATS

Named after a local eccentric, James Lucas, he was a local landowner who studied medicine. However, upon his mother's death in 1849 these eccentricities were greatly heightened. He refused to administer his mother's will, in which he inherited the family estate at nearby Redcoats Green, and delayed her funeral for several months.

He locked himself in his house, living solely in the kitchen on a diet of bread, cheese, eggs, herrings and gin, wearing only a blanket and sleeping in the ashes and soot of the fire. He never washed or cut his hair, which grew to waist-length.

Although he had locked himself away he was quite willing to receive visitors, including well-to-do people, who conversed with him.

He died in 1874 and after his death seventeen cartloads of dirt and ashes were removed from the house.

Titmore Green, Hertfordshire. A two-storey red-brick Victorian building, with multiple gables facing the road. Recently undergone a complete refurbishment which has removed the last vestige of Victoriana from the building.

HIBBERT ARMS

Hibbert Street, Luton, Bedfordshire Set in the old part of town, a two-storey mid-terraced building of grey and mellow brown bricks built in Victorian times (circa 1880), A cosy U-shaped bar which has a real fire and a small beer garden at the rear.

May be called after the British merchant and philanthropist, Robert Hibbert, 1769-1849, a Jamaican slave owner who founded the Hibbert Trust in 1847 which later financed the Hibbert Lectures from 1878. He bought the East Hide (Hyde) estate near Luton. Pub now called the Hibbert.

The swinging sign shows the Hibbert Crest.

HIGHWAYMAN

Dunstable, Bedfordshire. A modern pub built beside the A5 on the edge of town. Its name could refer to one of many highwaymen who haunted the area in times past, including a robber called Dunning, who reputedly had the town called after him.

HILL HOUSE

Happisburgh, Norfolk. (if you do not speak Norfolk it is pronounced 'Haysburra'). The pub takes its name from its altitude, which is not that great in comparison to other places. Remember Noel Coward's *Private Lives*? Very flat, Norfolk.

The original building dates from circa 1550 but was only licensed as a pub from 1610.

In one part of the bar there is a Sherlock Holmes corner with a few dedications to the man, the connection being that in 1905 Sir Arthur Conan Doyle wrote part of one of the *Sherlock Holmes* stories here which concerned a series of stick men used as a code. The idea was updated in a film of 1942, starring Basil Rathbone and Nigel Bruce. Legend has it that the idea came from the landlord's son, who had concocted the code.

One unusual feature of the pub is the signal box which has been converted to accommodation for guests. The story goes that in 1901 the village was going to have a railway station, so the railway company built the signal box in readiness for the line being laid; however, the railway never came…

HOOPS

The name could relate to a number of things; during the sixteenth and seventeenth centuries some quart pots were made from a number of hoops so that when a drink was shared you had a marker for your share. When I lived in Suffolk during the 1970s it was a common practice for one customer to offer another a drink from his glass with the bidding 'drink long and deep'. So the habit of sharing a drink still remained.

An earlier reference to 'hoops' could have been a sign showing that a new brew was on sale – similar to an ale stick. Sometimes these hoops were decorated with greenery. It was the forerunner to the habit of having the inn sign surrounded by a hoop.

In some parts of the country it is referring to the bird Hoopoe, which, through confusion, came to mean a Lapwing, as they both have a prominent crest. It is also an obsolete measure used for salt, grain, etc.

Bassingbourne, Hertfordshire. A late seventeenth century timber-framed and part-thatched two-storey building which at one time was two separate buildings. This is reflected in the layout of the pub, with one part being a quiet public bar with tiled floor and log fire, whilst the other end is a self-contained restaurant with roof and support beams.

The swinging sign shows a cooper fitting the hoops to a barrel.

HOPE AND ANCHOR

The anchor rates among the earliest of Christian symbols. Because of its great importance in keeping a boat steady in a storm, it was regarded by the ancients as a sign of hope and steadfastness. Hebrews 6:19-20 states: "As an anchor of the soul, sure and firm".

The anchor is a cross resting on a crescent moon, or bowl. The latter being a crude female symbol or representation of the womb. The intersecting lines on a cross represent the spirit and matter so indicates a person's thoughts and actions.

There is also a pub called this on Hope Cove in Devon; in this case the name seems to have been suggested by the location.

South Ferriby, Lincolnshire. Situated on the banks of the River Humber, the pub is a two-storey brick building which has had a varied life. In 1842 there was a pub in the village called the Ferry Boat, which seems to have closed down in 1868, and another called the Sloop opened the same year; this also seemed to have closed, this time in 1913. The present pub is called the 'Hope and Anchor'. But I cannot find out when this name came into being. I am sure in the late 1970s it was called the 'Sluice', as I used to visit it to buy smoked eels, there being an old chap who caught them in the River Ancholme and smoked them himself. They were delicious!

In 2013 the pub was swamped by a tidal surge and closed for eighteen months, which meant the pub had to be refurbished. The inside is now driftwood cladding with dark panelling along with a general sea-themed décor, consisting of a bar, dining room and conservatory with views over the River Humber.

Syston, Leicestershire. Haunted by a spirit called Benji, who has the most annoying habit of slamming doors or whistling loudly late at night; he also has a mischievous streak in him, as the barmaids complain that he pinches their bottoms. On the rare occasions he actually appears he is described as a thin transparent ghost.

HORSE AND CHAINS

Bushey, Hertfordshire. A seventeenth century coaching house known in 1698 as 'two cottages at the stump', the stump being the hitching post halfway up the hill where the horses were rested and fed while the passengers and coachmen no doubt had refreshment of their own. It was not until the last horse was retired in 1938 that the stables and horse trough were removed.

The bar is open-plan with a separate restaurant area and a small private room accessed through the bar which has low ceilings, bare beams and a log fire. The room has a ghostly presence that throws glasses about, thought to be a former landlord who haunted the building in the 1970s.

At one time called Snappers Fish Bar but returned to a traditional pub in 2007. The only pub of this name in the United Kingdom, it refers to days gone by when extra horses were attached by chains to coaches or wagons to assist them to climb steep inclines; such horses often had special shoes fitted to enable them to gain a greater grip.

HORSE AND GROOM

This was common name for a pub, especially close to where people kept their horses and carriages in towns and latterly close to racing stables. The sign may or may not celebrate a particular horse.

Barleythorpe, Leicestershire. This pub was owned by Hugh Cecil Lowther (Lord Lonsdale), because he thought his staff were spending too much time there, he closed it – as was possible to do during the inter-war period.

Known as the Yellow Earl, as nearly everything he owned was so coloured. He was founder and first president of the Automobile Association, who adopted his livery; he was also a great sportsman, known by some as 'England's greatest sporting gentleman'. It was he that donated the original 'Lonsdale Belts' in 1909 for boxing.

He died at Stud House, Barleythorpe, in 1944.

Melton, Suffolk.

The first mention of the pub was in 1842, when it was one of several auctioned, although the first licence was not issued until 1853, but this could have been for a full licence, having been only a beer house previously.

One source tells that it had been a coaching house, another that it only had a beer licence, a coach stop would need more than just ale for its customers. Perhaps the 1853 licence was when it became a coaching house, as the old road from Ipswich to Lowestoft may have passed through the village. It certainly appeared to on a map of 1776, although somewhat indistinct.

The following tale was told by the landlord's son, which goes like this; on one dark night, Goodman Kemp of Woodbridge came into the inn requesting loan of a gun in order to shoot a 'shock' which he had seen by the gate. Kemp, with a companion, then attempted to grab the creature, having in mind to take it into the inn for a good look. As he seized it, the creature had bitten him on the hand before vanishing. Kemp showed the marks to prove it. This would have been late eighteenth to early nineteenth century, and the 'shock' referred to was a goblin in the shape of a dog which haunted footpaths and byways at night.

This is another pub which closed in December 2009 and is now a private residence.

HORSE AND JOCKEY

Waddington, Lincolnshire. Sixteenth century coaching house which is a Grade I listed building.

Haunted by the green lady but no other information available. (It makes a change from the ubiquitous 'Grey Lady').

Swinging sign shows a jockey leading his horse.

HUTT

The original name was given as told below; this was just the medieval spelling of the modern word. There were other 'hutts', mostly run by wives of tradesmen or labourers for the benefit of travellers, such as the drovers who traversed the country. Generally they would have been little more than a hut but would supply food and overnight accommodation for such travellers. Later some of these would perhaps expand into coaching houses depending where they were situated.

Ravenshead, Nottinghamshire. Fifteenth century stone and brick, built on the site of King John's 'Royal Hutt', where the foresters who protected the royal deer were housed. By the seventeenth century it had become a coaching inn, where travellers would gather before setting out on the road through what was called 'Thieves Wood'.

It is a most magnificent building, with front facing gables and even the dormer having one, along with mullioned windows, which have an almost church-like look about them.

There is reputed to be a mile-long tunnel built by the monks which connects the pub with nearby Newstead Abbey, this would have been a handy escape route for the priests if attacked, or perhaps an underground route for clandestine meetings with the barmaid!

One of a national chain of pub/eating houses.

The swinging sign show an ancient hut with a privy beside it.

There is a story regarding 'Thieves Wood', in 1883 a gamekeeper called Albert Spinks shot a bird he did not know. He showed it to a local naturalist, Joseph Whitaker, who recognised it as an Egyptian nightjar; he had it stuffed and this is now in a museum. The next sighting of this rare bird was in 1984.

The only plagues of London are the immoderate drinking of fools and the frequency of fires.

William Fitzstephen, 1173, in his prologue to 'Life of Becket'.

IVY HOUSE

Ivy was the plant of Bacchus the Roman God of Wine, so it is not surprising that a number of pubs continued the custom of naming a drinking establishment after him, although the tradition has waned rather in the past centuries. Folklore has it if you make an infusion of ivy and drink it you will not get drunk. You try it. I'm not going to!

Chalfont St Giles, Buckinghamshire. Haunted by a Victorian couple who wander through the hotel as if they own the place.

> All you that bring tobacco here must pay for pipes as well as beer,
> And you that stand before the fire, I pray sit down by good desire
> That other folks as well as you may see the fire and feel it too.
> Since man to man is so unjust, I cannot tell what man to trust;
> My liquor's good, 'tis no man's sorrow: pay today, I'll trust tomorrow.

Anon.

JACKAL

Thurleigh, Bedfordshire. A rather odd building; one section is a mostly single-storey heavy thatched building, whilst the other half is a more modern two-storey. The old cottage part dates from at least 1656, when it was mortgaged by a tailor for £8. It was first known as a public house in 1817, when it was called the Trefoil or Fleur de Lis, and it appears the cottage was joined to the modern building by this time. In 1832, when, once again, the pub changed hands, the name was also changed to the Jackal.

How it came by that name is a mystery, as not too many people in the early nineteenth century, would have seen a Jackal. It may, be the landlord chose the name simply because it *would* draw interest.

The swinging sign showed a black-backed Jackal; it was the only pub of this name in the United Kingdom.

At the time of writing the pub is closed and its future uncertain.

JENYNS ARMS

Downham Market, Norfolk. This nineteenth century pub is on the banks of the River Great Ouse, close to the bridge over the Denver Sluice. Here tolls were levied on almost everything; the few exemptions were officials of the Great Ouse River Board or locals attending church on Sunday. Inside the inn is displayed a list of former toll charges and payments which were only discontinued in 1963.

The pub takes its name from George Leonard Jenyns, who was an English priest. In 1787 he inherited Bottisham Hall and a considerable fortune; that same year he became vicar at nearby Swaffham Prior.

Later he became chairman of the Bedford Level Corporation and also served on the Board of Agriculture.

The Bedford Level Corporation was set up in 1630 to drain much of the fens by cutting two channels with retaining banks and building pumping stations to raise the water. In exchange for putting up the money to finance the work, those who did would be rewarded with parcels of land which consisted of four thousand acres for each £500 share.

The two channels are still in use today, being the New Bedford River and the Hundred Foot Drain; they run parallel with each other for almost twenty miles with the land separating the two rivers being below sea level so it can flood when required.

The swinging sign shows the arms of the Jenyns, but the motto '*Ignaus Nunquam*' does not seem to make sense in Latin.

JOHN GILPIN

John Gilpin was a comic ballad written in 1782 by William Cowper (1731-1800) which describes the antics of Gilpin, who had borrowed a horse to ride to the Bell at Edmonton, as the coach he had hired was full with his family. The horse would not obey his commands and gradually ran faster and faster going past the Bell, not stopping until it reached its master's house in Ware.

When Gilpin tried to coax the horse back to the Bell a similar thing happened; the horse would not stop until it reached London.

It starts;

John Gilpin was a citizen
Of credit and renown.
A train-band captain eke was he
Of famous London town.

John Gilpins spouse said to her dear,
'Though wedded we have been
These twice ten tedious years, yet we
No holiday have seen.

'To-morrow is our wedding day,
And we will then repair
Unto the Bell at Edmonton,
All in a chaise and pair.

There are fifty verses telling of this journey.

Ware, Hertfordshire. The original inn of this name was first known in 1868 and stood a short distance from the modern pub. The old Gilpin is now a private house.

A new pub was built in 1969 on the site of the Malakoff pub, the licence of the Red House was also relinquished in order to obtain the new licence.

It was a two-bar pub with a garden.

It closed in October 2014, now awaiting demolition and redevelopment into a housing site.

Another unique pub name bites the dust!

A note on the word Jolly; as inn signs progressed from a bush to other more sophisticated forms, mythology became popular, with Bacchus, the god of wine and ecstatic liberation, becoming an obvious choice for a pub sign. Landlords who were out to entice customers into their premises used the word 'Jolly' added to the name as an indication that their pub was a place for entertainment as well as for drinking. In due time the word became associated with many different trades, all implying a good time could be had at that inn, possibly with other tradesmen of the same occupation. As all this changed when the Puritans were in charge, as mentioned in the preface.

JOLLY ANGLERS

Beeston, Nottinghamshire. A large two-storey brick and stone pub, built in 1937 as a replacement for another pub of the same name close by. The old pub was in existence from at least 1855. They both serviced the community which grew up around the canal.

The swinging sign shows three happy anglers.

JOLLY HIGGLERS

These were wandering pedlars who exchanged poultry and dairy produce in the town for commodities which they then sold in the country. Higgle is a Scottish word meaning to argue, particularly in bargaining. Haggle is more frequently used today.

Nottingham, Nottinghamshire. The earlier beer house was trading at least as early as 1825. A new traditional two-floor building with a single-storey extension was built on the same site during the late 1960s or early 1970s when the area was redeveloped. By 2013 it had been turned into a convenience store.

The original building was a large three-storey brick-built corner pub with a curved flat roof at one end extending round the corner, with the entrance actually on the corner.

The name was probably taken from the water deliverers of the eighteenth century onwards. The area where the pub stood had at one time a pumping station which raised water from two wells which was then carted around town by 'water higglers' selling at ½ penny a bucketful.

Yet another pub name hits the dust. The only pub I can find with this name.

JOLLY SAILOR

A traditional sign at many a port where sailors who had spent months or even years at sea could be tempted to be parted from their money. Nearly always either on or very close to a quay.

Sometimes they had verses such as;

"Curl up your rope and anchor here,
'Til better weather does appear."

Orford, Suffolk. Built sometime between the end of the sixteenth century and the middle of the seventeenth century, reputedly using wood from shipwrecks. This is quite probable as the timbers of ships were a valuable source of building material.

Being only a short distance from the quay, the pub's association with smuggling is a foregone conclusion, especially as one old source tells that the pub was full of secret cupboards.

In the late nineteenth century, an Orford seaman brought back three tiny 'muff' dogs from China which were on show in the pub for a while. This particularly small breed was carried inside a lady's muff to keep her hands warm.

The swinging sign shows a rather comic sailor dressed in red and white bell bottoms with a blue blazer, wearing his cutlass and carrying a caged parrot.

JOLLY WAGGONERS

Innkeepers were also agents for picking up and dropping off goods by wagon companies, though these generally tended to avoid inns favoured by coaches. They served the local community as a dropping off and collection point for all kinds of things, including at one time mail, prior to the national mail system being implemented.

Ardeley, Hertfordshire. The buildings were constructed in the sixteenth century as farmworkers' cottages. First called the 'New Bell Inn', as it stood next to the 'Old Bell'.

In front of the pub stood a blacksmith's forge, so farm implements, carts and horses used to wait in front of the pub until it was their turn (no doubt the owners were inside the pub). One waggoner was so infamous that the pub was named after him.

JOLLY WOODMAN

Burnham Beeches, Buckinghamshire. A typical Georgian two-storey, red-brick, square building with a smaller two-storey extension build on one side. It was granted a licence in 1832, which makes it the oldest pub in the village.

The pub has been used in various films ranging from a *Carry On* (when it was, of course, called The Cock) to *Genevieve*, and TV's *Midsomer Murders*. In 2014 it was winner of Pubs in Bloom.

The pub name is quite apt for the area, as Burnham Beeches is famous for the beech trees growing there, so a woodman would have found plenty of work felling the trees for the chair-making in nearby High Wycombe.

The swinging sign shows a woodman holding an axe and a pint of beer.

JUDES FERRY

West Row, Suffolk. The pub has had a variety of names over the years; it was a pub from at least 1844 and was known as the Ferry House in 1855, The Ferry from 1865 until 1912 when it became known as Judes Ferry House.

I have not been able to solve the mystery of the name, as none of the landlords I can trace, had the name Jude.

The hanging sign shows a man punting a young woman across the River Lark.

JUMPS INN

Marston Moretaine, Bedfordshire. Named after a local tradition, which tells of a farmer playing 'Jumps', probably leapfrog, on a Sunday. The Devil appeared and leapt from the church tower to land on the Jump Stone, a standing stone about two feet high, from where he carried the Sabbath breaker away. The same tale is told of three lads, who 'all vanished in a blue flame'.

Yet another version of the tale tells the Devil took a giant leap from the top of the church tower, landing in a nearby field. He then took a second leap which landed him close to a pub called The Leaps; a third jump took him to a gang of lads playing leapfrog, which he joined. He tricked them into jumping down a hole into his kingdom and they were never seen again. A boulder called the 'Devil's Jump Stone' now marks the place where the boys disappeared. The pub changed its name to The Jumps but was demolished in the 1930s.

> Drink here and drown all sorrow;
> Pay today, I'll trust tomorrow.
>
> *Anon.*

KING'S ARMS

Occasionally you can date the pub by which arms they show; although as they can change even for the same monarch, this is not always a reliable test.

Sandy, Bedfordshire. Built on the site of an old morgue, so it not surprising the pub is haunted by several shades. One likes to throw beer barrels about in the cellar, whilst another enjoys pitching carpentry nails at the customers.

KING'S HEAD

There was a courtier's joke regarding pubs called by this name. When asking advice on which inn to stay, they were often told 'the Lord's Arms is always full, but the King's Head is usually empty'. Of course this was never said in front of anyone other than trusted friends, otherwise you may end up a head shorter yourself!

Aylesbury, Buckinghamshire. In King's Head Passage off the Market Square. One of the oldest and best-preserved coaching houses in the country, on the road from London to Bicester. It carries the Royal Arms of Henry VI and his queen, Margaret of Anjou, together with those of Prince Edward, who died at the Battle of Tewkesbury.

A monastery gatehouse dating from 1455 with timber framing, it is entered through a medieval gateway to a central cobbled courtyard with the original stabling. In the lounge there is a magnificent wooden-framed leaded window, old when the Tudors came to the throne, which contained twenty panes of fifteenth century stained glass; two panes are now part of a window in Westminster Abbey and three others are in the British Museum – there can't be too much of it left! The Great Hall of the inn also has fifteenth century stained-glass mullions. Other items of interest are a section of exposed wattle and daub, and a chair in the lounge reputedly used by Cromwell, for it is thought he stayed here in 1651 after his victory at the Battle of Worcester. During the Civil War, the town was the base for both King and Parliament, according to which way the battle was going.

The building with cobbled courtyard and original stabling now belongs to the National Trust and has been gently restored.

There is the King's Head Festival held in July.

The inn is haunted by a grey lady who appears by the chimney of the great hall; another ghost is what is thought to have been a cleaner in the pub who died circa 1900.

A third shows up in the basement as a man dressed in a dated suit; all seem to be harmless.

KING'S OAK

High Beach, Hertfordshire. There are two ways of spelling the place name; some spell it Beach; others, Beech. It seems that the place takes its name from a large sandy area nearby, so the spelling Beach seems more appropriate.

Constructed in 1887, it is a three-storey Victorian monstrosity of a building with what appears to be several single-storey 'add-ons', one of which has iron railings round it as if it were a balcony, except there is no obvious access apart from climbing through a window.

Outside it has a garden with a children's play area and, unusually, an outdoor swimming pool which is open during the summer; there are also some picnic tables at the front of the building.

The swinging sign show what appears to a be a pair of open wings with a scroll underneath, surmounted by a crown.

The hotel is supposedly named after the oak under which Henry VIII is said to have sat while Anne Boleyn was being executed in London in 1536. Was he too busy canoodling with Jane Seymour to attend?

KING WILLIAM IV

William IV, 1765-1837, was the third son of George III who joined the navy as midshipman in 1779; he quickly became a captain. As he was known to disobey orders and violate discipline, he was never given command of a ship. So why he was later appointed Admiral of the Fleet in 1801 seems a little odd.

St Albans, Hertfordshire. Although it was only built in 1937, the pub is haunted by a six-foot-tall officer in military uniform with green buttons on his tunic. Before the pub was built the site was occupied by a drill hall used by the local militia. The pub was formerly called the Jim Thompson.

KNIGHTS LODGE

Corby, Northamptonshire. A seventeenth century two-storey inn built of local limestone that has a slate roof. In the first Queen Elizabeth's reign, the building was called the Lawnde [sic] Lodge, as it stood on the Lawn of Benfield. She granted custody of the lawn and lodge to Sir Christopher Hatton; on his death in 1591 his cousin, also Christopher Hatton, inherited the lodge. This is where the name of Knights Lodge may have come from, although another source tells that it was a lodging house for knights before Elizabethan times. Despite its age, the building only became a pub in 1967.

Inside the pub is open-plan with a long single room that has a log fire at one end. The pub has rather a lot of ghostly happenings; barmaids are particularly at risk, having their skirts lifted, their bottoms pinched and their thighs tickled with what they are sure is a quill! Other apparitions include a cavalier, complete with ostrich feather in his hat, girls giggling and gossiping, footfalls on the staircase, and a short-lived shadowy figure who quickly evaporates. One of the spooks gets physical at times; a workman refused to finish a job as he was constantly being pushed about when he was alone in the room. Finally there is the smell of lilies on the stairs, even out of season – the stairs are where a young girl fell and was killed many years ago.

> If all be true that I do think
> There are five reasons we should drink:
> Good wine, a friend, or being dry,
> Or lest we should be by and by,
> Or any other reason why.
>
> *'Reasons for Drinking'; Henry Aldrich, 1647-1710*

LADY OF THE LAKE

In Arthurian legend the Lady of the Lake is the titular name of the ruler of Avalon, which is a lake where she is surrounded by knights and damsels – one legend has it that this was Dozmary Pool on Bodmin Moor; another gives the location as being near Glastonbury.

She features in many of the tales, ranging from giving Arthur the sword Excalibur to rearing Lancelot and the seduction of Merlin. She has many and diverse names depending on which story you read. In Sir Walter Scott's poem 'The Lady of the Lake', she is Ellen Douglas, who lived with her outlawed father Lord James near Loch Katrine in the Trossachs of Scotland.

LAKESIDE INN

Oulton Broad, Suffolk. Previously called the Lake. The swinging sign has nothing to do with Arthurian legend – this shows a ship in full sail. A reminder, perhaps, of when Lowestoft was a busy port.

LAMB

A lamb, apart from being an animal, is a religious sign in Christianity and the Jewish faith. A white lamb is a sign of innocence and purity; in John 1:29 it is said, "Behold the Lamb of God, which takes away the sins of the world".

It was referring to Jesus Christ, who sacrificed himself to save mankind.

The sign was also used by the Knights Templar and Merchant Taylors as part of their coat of arms. In earlier days it was a sign that food and accommodation could be had by pilgrims usually at a monastic house. It was one of the earliest signs for an inn.

The sign was particularly popular in sheep-breeding areas where the local economy relied on the animals.

Berkhamsted, Hertfordshire. A two-storey whitewashed brick pub with tiled roof, which is over three hundred years old. There are two 'rooms', each with a front door, connected by a narrow section in front of the bar. Both rooms have low ceilings with oak beams and at one end a wood-burner; the seating is mixed, with some high chairs, but predominantly traditional bench and chairs. The décor is photographs of the old town, sometimes with the pub featured.

At the rear is a patio which is reached through a stained-glass-panelled door and there are some picnic tables at the front of the building.

The hanging sign shows a lamb in a half barrel.

LAMPLIGHTER'S (HALL)

Leicester, Leicestershire. The pub was set up in the late 1980s and takes the name because it was in the old gas offices, now called the Firebug.

The building is a two-storey building constructed of bright red and rose pink-coloured bricks, and is quite startling.

The round swinging sign showed an old lamplighter doing his rounds.

LAND OF LIBERTY, PEACE AND PLENTY

The name 'Peace and Plenty' for inns evolved because landlords allowed his midday customers a free kebbuck-end, the remains of a cheese, and a scone with their refreshments. This was a well-established custom in many places in both Scotland and England, it only disappeared in the early days of the Kaiser's war in 1914.

Heronsgate, Hertfordshire. Built in the 1820s, it was first a beer house frequented by drovers on the way to markets at Watford and Rickmansworth. It became a pub in 1870.

Inside it is a single room with wooden floors and ceiling beams. It is the décor which attracts the eye though; a framed collection of beer mats, some from long-gone breweries; mirrors advertising a brewery; and, of course, the ubiquitous pump clips, as well as a fair selection of bottled beers. Definitely a pub dedicated to beer drinkers!

Outside there is a large grassed garden with a covered, heated part called the 'Pavilion' along with picnic tables at the front.

This pub name originated from the aspirations of a commune established nearby in 1846 by Fergus O'Connor, a Chartist MP, along with the Chartist Cooperative Land Company. Their aim was to resettle industrial workers from the cities on smallholdings which made them both independent of factory bosses while at the same time becoming potential voters. Until the Great Reform Act of 1832 only landowners were allowed the vote – after that time the urban middle classes were allowed the vote. (It was not until 1918 that all males over twenty-one were allowed to vote. The act also included women over thirty who were landowners)

Land was bought after a public subscription was run, and the thirty-five plots were allocated by ballot on Easter Monday 1846. It was to be called the O'Connorville Estate.

One reference tells that the pub has altered its name to Land of Liberty; however, the wall signs and the swinging one all state Land of Liberty, Peace and Plenty.

The swinging sign has two differing pictures; on one side there is King John signing the Magna Carta and on the other two Victorian politicians addressing a rally.

LEA GATE INN

Coningsby, Lincolnshire. Survives from the sixteenth century, situated in the Lincolnshire Fens, it is believed to be the last remaining 'guide house' in the fens. This inn's name recalls a former tollgate close by.

In earlier days before the fens were drained, when passage across them was not always safe, it was important for travellers to keep to the turnpike roads. Travellers approaching the inn at night found their way by keeping in sight the glowing torch fixed to the gable of the pub in an iron holder, still to be seen projecting from the wall. The same guiding light was employed in many isolated inns, especially where the ground could be treacherous.

The Lea Gate stands in an enclosure known as Gibbet Nook Close. The site of the gibbet being in the present beer garden by the yew tree, which is estimated as being older than the inn.

Laurence Eusden/Eusdon, Poet Laureate, rector in the eighteenth century, was a regular customer and known to enjoy his pint, being referred to as 'the drunken parson' by Thomas Gray, a poet of a somewhat better stamp.

Members of a RAF base nearby accounted for custom. One of the pilots borrowed the sign during WWII, 'to show to the Germans', but he never returned and neither did the sign. Its place over the front door is still empty.

LEVIATHAN

Originally a Biblical sea monster identified as a crocodile or a whale; also equated with Satan, depending which books of the Bible you read. From the early nineteenth century it has meant anything of a huge size or aspect.

Watford, Hertfordshire. The railway came to Watford in 1837 and this inn opened a year later with a name appropriate to the newcomer's large size. It was, for a time, called the Leviathan Steamer, the Steamer later being dropped; it then became The Champion, then the Sycamore and is now called the Prince George.

This was the only pub of this name in the United Kingdom.

LILLEY ARMS

Lilley, Hertfordshire. The building dates from 1705; it was originally a coaching house on the main road to the east-being just about halfway between Luton and Hitchen.

First called the Sugarloaf, in 1852 it changed to the Sowerby Arms, which was the name of the local lord of the manor. It then changed to the Lilley Arms during WWI. Has a number of old gas lamps for illumination outside.

There are several resident ghosts; one 'Old Tom' who makes regular appearances is a former landlord, Tom Connisbee, who has his own chair in the bar. Another is a friend of Tom's, a lady called Frances Mitchell who owned a millinery business nearby. Others include an eighteenth century postman, a lady called Rose Ann and a child who plays in the orchard, to name but a few.

The swinging sign shows the arms of the village which incorporates what else but- three lilies.

LIMEBURNERS

Offton, Suffolk. Built possibly as late as the 1850s to slake the thirst of the workers in the lime kilns opposite the pub, at a reputed cost of £800. The pub was previously named the Limeburners Arms, but I was not told when the change took place. In the 1960s when I visited, a game was played here that had a fascinating way of combining darts and cribbage: segments on the dartboard were marked five, ten and fifteen, plus the traditional doubles and trebles. Five scores one hole, ten scores two, etc. The score was marked on a cribbage board and you must finish on a double. Not as easy as it sounds!

The pub was closed in 2006 due to water damage and its future was in doubt; fortunately repairs were carried out and it is back in business again.

A swinging sign shows two men on top of a lime kiln.

LION

A lion has appeared on Royal Coats of Arms since William the Conqueror and is shown on signboards alongside an assortment of other animals and objects.

Buckden, Cambridgeshire. A sixteenth century coaching inn formerly called the Lion and Lamb, thought to have been built about 1492. It was possibly the guest house for the Palace of the Bishops of Lincoln. The great hall of this medieval building dates from the same time and has a unique timbered ceiling, where rafters meet in a central boss carved with the symbol of the lamb. An inscription in black letters reads: '*Ecce Agnus Dei*' – ('Behold the Lamb of God'). Its wide hearth has a huge beam, moulded and carved with roses at each end. Because of its ecclesiastical connection, it was first called the Lamb of God.

Although the name changed during coaching days, the inn is still known locally as the Lion and Lamb. Both names appear over the door.

The swinging sign shows a white lion *passant guardant* on a black background, with the name below in reversed colours.

LION REVIVED

Bulwell, Nottinghamshire. Mid-nineteenth-century two-storey stone 'cube' with a flat roof, although, parts of the rear of the building date from early 1700s, when it was called Bulwell Spring. The present building was called White Lion, then The Robinson Hill Social Club, then, finally, circa 1975, Lion Revived.

Haunted by the ghost of an elderly gentleman wearing a cap. The hanging sign is plain white lettering on black background.

LIONS AT BLEDLOW

Bledlow, Buckinghamshire. A seventeenth early eighteenth century whitewashed brick single-storey with attics and a tiled roof. It has a small twentieth century extensions at the left-hand side and a larger one at the rear. There are low-beamed interconnecting rooms around a central bar with a large brick inglenook, uneven stone floors, ceiling beams and high-backed settles.

Has featured several times in the TV programme *Midsomer Murders*.

The Grey Lady, a resident ghost, appears in the cellars or an upstairs passageway but is friendly; sadly it is not known who she is.

Opposite is a small green which has picnic tables on it.

The swinging sign shows two lions one above the other, going in different directions on a cream background.

LITTLE ABBEY HOTEL

Great Missenden, Buckinghamshire. Now a conference centre and hotel, a part-Tudor building which still shows traces of its ecclesiastical past, having an ancient carved cross above the entrance.

Missenden Abbey was founded in 1133 for the Augustine Order; it became one of the largest and richest abbey's in the county.

The Little Abbey became a convent for nuns and gained its independence from Missenden in 1188. A legend persists that a passage connected it to Missenden Abbey, about half a mile distant-which today is a college for adult education. This passage was believed to have been used by monks when they came to administer sacraments to their spiritual sisters, but scandals suggested its use was more worldly.

Its existence has been doubted, but a trapdoor was discovered in the centre of the hotel's breakfast-room floor, which has since been sealed.

In 1286, the Abbot of Missenden tried to trick one Nicholas the Taverner into signing away his inn while he lay ill in the Abbey. A canon was sent to make his wife leave the building so monks could take possession, but she refused, thinking it odd, so stayed until her husband could return to his property.

During 1292 a young monk was found breaking Abbey rules involving a nun. So strict was the rule at that time that he was driven to cut his throat for fear of the discipline; it is his ghost which haunts the Little Abbey Hotel today.

The Abbey was dissolved in 1539 and the Little Abbey passed into private hands. Alteration and additions during the last centuries include a delightful minstrel's gallery which overlooks the dining room, and it is near this gallery guests have heard sounds believed to be echoes from the unfortunate young monk.

LIVE AND LET LIVE

According to the OED the saying means 'to be tolerant of others and be so tolerated'. During the rise of Methodism and teetotalism, when many were trying to stop others drinking alcohol, such a name would have flourished. There are no doubt many other instances where the name is appropriate.

Pegsdon, Bedfordshire. Eighteenth century building which has been much extended and recently been refurbished, and now contains several restaurants.

Story has it that the pub takes its name from a tale of two hundred years ago. The local landowners were suffering a spate of poaching, so they arranged for the Bow Street Runners to catch the culprits. They surrounded the pub at Pegsdon where the gang were planning their next foray. Finding themselves trapped, they agreed to stop poaching on condition they were allowed to go free, which the Runners agreed to. The landlord, impressed by this attitude, immediately changed the name of the pub.

There is a huge garden with picnic tables, overlooking the Pegsdon Hills. The swinging sign is plain, with a black running deer on a green background.

LOBSTER SMACK

Canvey Island, Essex. Situated on the south-west coast of the island, snuggled under the sea wall, this pub is a Grade II listed building.

One reference tells that a pub has been on this site since 1600; this is unlikely, as the island was prone to regular flooding until the Dutch dyke builders in about 1623 made sea defences and drained the island, reclaiming 3,600 acres of land on the promise of being given one third for themselves. That is why many street names on the island are Dutch.

Another states the pub was built in the 1600s. This seems more likely, as it would have been constructed after the flood defences – or perhaps during the latter stages of construction – possibly to service the workers.

It was rebuilt in 1700s as Worlds End which, considering the position, was a very apt name; later it became the Sluice House, then Lobster Pot, before finishing with Lobster Smack.

Because of its isolation the pub was renowned for the bare-knuckle boxing that took place during the 1850s. Again, due to its isolated position, it was an obvious haunt for smugglers or, as one source tells. of pirates. However, they did not get it all their own way; the Revenue built several wooden houses to home a squad of men who were stationed on the island.

Lastly, it is probable this pub Charles Dickens described as the Sluice where Pip and Magwitch stayed overnight before attempting to catch a mail boat for the continent.

LOLLARDS PIT

Norwich, Norfolk. John Wycliffe was a fourteenth century theologian who believed the church was in many ways corrupt; he preached the replacement of the present rich opulent hierarchy with priests who lived in poverty. He was an early believer in Protestant Reformation and a believer in the Bible being translated into English instead of Latin.

The pub takes its name from a pit over which the pub has been built. It had once been a quarry just outside the city walls where followers of Wycliffe were burnt at the stake.

Formerly called the Kings Arms until 1975, then the Bridge House until 2012, when the present name was adopted.

LONG BOW

Nottingham, Nottinghamshire. A post-war single-storey building which has a steep pitched tiled roof with windows set into it; also a single storey with a tiled roof.

An apt name for a pub, considering the legend of Robin Hood and his merry men, who lived in the nearby forest, all of whom carried longbows.

LONGE ARMS

Spixworth, Norfolk. A 1930s pub, named after John Longe, who was lord of the manor in the mid-1800s.

This pub at one time, did have a very unusual ghost. A phantom woman would wait outside the pub until a person known as 'old John' came out. She would then walk beside him until he was safely home. After he died she was never seen again, although story has it you can hear her crying in the lanes on a stormy night.

LYTTON ARMS

Robert Lytton was one of Henry VII's favourites, for whom Knebworth House was built, a Tudor mansion dating from 1492 and standing in its own park.

Sir Edward Bulwer-Lytton, the novelist, 1803-73, and his descendant remodelled the house in the 1840s.

The Baronetcy was created 1838 for Edward (George Earle Lytton) Bulwer-Lytton, 1st Baron Lytton. Born 1803, he was deputy lieutenant for Hertfordshire and MP for various constituencies from 1831 onwards.

Knebworth, Hertfordshire. An early Victorian symmetrical two-storey four-gabled brick building; the outer gables extend to cover the two bay windows on the first floor.

Beneath, on the ground floor are four bay windows, with a door on either side of the centre two. The present building was constructed in 1887, but the post office directory indicates that there was a pub on the site five years earlier.

Inside the room is open-plan, roughly U-shaped with two areas set for dining. The carpeted one has a wood burner along with a pair of high-back settles facing one another, making a private booth. The other, with a tiled floor, leads into a heated marquee on the sheltered patio which has picnic tables – there are also some at the front of the building.

The bar has a wooden floor, a large brick-built fire surround and a plain ceiling. The swinging sign show the arms of the Lytton family but without a motto.

Wine that gladdens human hearts.

Psalm 104:15

MAD CAT

Pidley, Cambridgeshire. Dating from 1648. Legend has it that years ago when the pub was called the White Lion a new sign was commissioned; when it arrived it was so poorly painted that the locals thought it looked more like a mad cat. The name stuck. Ironically, despite the name, all dogs are welcome.

The hanging sign shows a smiling cat's face.

MAD DOG

Little Odell, Bedfordshire. The two-storey pub is constructed, as most of the of the village is, from limestone rubble. The landowners were the Alston family, who also owned the Odell Castle Estate; they sold the pub to a local brewer in 1926 when the rent had been £40 per annum, a rise of ten pounds from 1918.

A story is that in 1724, a regular customer – Dr Richard Mead, physician and poisons expert, found himself without money to pay his bill, so he gave the landlord a recipe which told how to cure the bite of a mad dog. A strange alternative, but it was apparently accepted and the inn called the Mad Dog thereafter. What is was before we are not told. Sadly this story is only that – a story – as the pub did not exist until over a hundred years later, being licensed as late as 1831 when the licensee did advertise a cure for a mad dog's bite, hence the name. A further folk tale relates that a landlord named his pub Mad

Dog as many of his customers suffered from hydrophobia or, as he put it, an irrational fear of water.

When the bar ceiling was repaired in 1986, behind it was found a photograph of a young woman marked with an address in Colchester and dated to the 1870s. It was thought it might be a landlord's daughter who left the district to have an illegitimate child which was sent home to be looked after at the inn, but the portrait has been said not to resemble her.

An alternative story says a stranger coming to the pub saw the photograph and identified the woman as Margaret Bowden, a Victorian shrew known to frequent pubs who picked out customers to rob. She would leave, await her victim and then kill the unsuspecting person for their money or valuables. She was eventually caught and hanged.

Other curious things have been known to happen. Gas taps turn themselves off, items leap from the walls and locals have reported seeing a grey shape by the fire. The landlord's children, too, have felt something pass them in the upstairs passage.

Who is it, I wonder, that haunts the Mad Dog; Margaret Bowden or one of her victims? And if not either...

The pub is now a private house.

MAGPIE

It was thought to be a bird that brings omens depending on the number seen in a flock, as the children's nursery rhyme testifies; one for sorrow, two for mirth, three for a funeral, four for birth, five for heaven, etc.

A magpie is quite wrapped up in folklore far more than any other bird. In some areas of the country it is customary the greet a magpie and ask after his wife, others to spit over your shoulder three times. Some further greetings are less polite, as the one from Suffolk, which goes; "Hello, magpie, you thieving sod. Where's your fellow jailbird?" Alluding to the fact that magpies are usually seen in pairs and are thought to steal bright things.

There was an inn in the Strand during the reign of James I called Magotty Pie after the medieval name for the bird.

Stapleford, Nottinghamshire. A two-storey fairly modern brick pub with a single storey that has a tiled extension at either end.

The pub has a skittles alley and a function room. Outside is a beer garden and children's play area with patios on the front and the side of the building.

The hanging sign is plain writing.

MAID'S HEAD

Normally the sign shows a young girl's head – usually a dairymaid – but the OED says that the name also applies to a young skate or thornback-also a twait shad, although I cannot see many pubs using one of those for its sign.

Norwich, Norfolk. Originally owned by the bishops in the days of William the Conqueror and dating from Norman times, so already old when Queen Elizabeth I slept there in 1587. It stands in Tombland, where the city's first regular stagecoach to London, the Norwich Machine, left from in 1762. Tombland has nothing to do with cemeteries: it comes from the Anglo-Saxon 'tom', meaning 'empty', and this empty space was the town market-place until the present site in Peter's Street came into use after the Norman conquest.

The inn is mentioned in the Paston Letters, written by the eponymous English family from Paston in Norfolk that lived from the fourteenth to the seventeenth century. Only published between 1787 and 1823, these shed vivid light on domestic life from those centuries.

The ghost of an elderly man, believed to be a former mayor of the town, has been seen in the courtyard; also the shade of a maid has been reported, whose presence is detected by a musty smell of lavender.

Wicken, Cambridgeshire. In the lounge bar is an arrow cut into the wall above the fireplace. It was put there by Richard Fielder, an undergraduate at Jesus College, Cambridge, in the mid-nineteenth century. He spent his days fighting, drinking and scrawling doggerel verse on the walls of all the pubs he visited. At Wicken, a list can be seen of the places where these could at one time be read.

The arrow symbol used to appear in many Fenland homes. It indicated that visitors were welcome to food, drink and warmth but should not expect to stay the night.

This could well be patrin, a sign language used by the Romany to impart information to other members of the travelling clan. The pub was destroyed by fire in 1983 but rebuilt in the original design.

Initially a fifteenth century 'Hall House', the pub dates from the 1760s.

A swinging sign shows a picture of a dairymaid with a yoke across her shoulders and the name in a semi-circle above.

MAGNA CARTA

Lincoln, Lincolnshire. Dating from the nineteenth century, this building replaced half-timbered ones that were originally on the site. At the turn of the twentieth century the building housed a café and remained so until the 1950s, when it became a private residence for a number of years. The building then reverted to a café until converted to a pub in 1993.

The pub takes its name from one of only four copies of the *Magna Carta*, one of which is on display in the nearby castle.

The address has an exquisite name of No. 1 Exchequer Gate and is situated almost in the Minster Yard.

The hanging sign shows a scroll with seal and quill.

MALLARD

The famous steam engine which set a world speed record of 126 mph in 1938 between Grantham and Peterborough. Some signs depict the engine; others, the colourful male wild duck.

Ashby Decoy, Scunthorpe, Lincolnshire. A modern 1960s two-storey, brick, estate pub which retained the two-bar system, now more of a restaurant. Takes its name from the ducks that were once netted there. Ashby Décoy in former years was all marshland, once called Fritton Fen, which stretched to the River Trent. The area was renowned for the number of ducks that inhabited the area. It had been recorded in the late 1800s to have taken four thousand brace of duck in one season. The method was to use a trained dog. The animal would attract the attention of the ducks then run inside a tapering funnel-shaped netting, jump out at a discrete point, then return unseen to the ducks and again do the same; run inside the trap. This was done as many times as necessary until the inquisitive ducks followed the dog into the trap; meanwhile. a man would be feeding the ducks with a small amount of wheat. When sufficient birds were inside, the net was closed when the hunters could dispatch the trapped ducks at their leisure.

I am assured this was the way the ducks were trapped by an old gentleman whose grandfather was one of those licensed to take the game in this way, and the figures come from the game book which his grandfather kept.

This sign is of the male duck in all his colourful plumage. Now, I believe, closed.

MALT SHOVEL

A malt shovel was not a traditional metal one you use for coal or sand. It is a broad, flat piece of wood with the centre hollowed out to form the shovel shape; the handle was spliced on to this without any metal being used. I think the reasoning behind this was that at one time it was thought iron tainted the malt.

Ashby, Scunthorpe, Lincolnshire. This building has had a chequered career; it has been a shop, a cinema and a snooker hall. Now it is a comfortable bar fitted out with beams, along with furniture that has floral-patterned covers, with the added attraction of having a snooker hall attached.

There is no traditional hanging sign but there is a wall-mounted one showing what else… but a malt shovel.

MANVERS ARMS

Radcliffe on Trent, Nottinghamshire. Owned by the Earl of Manvers. The cellars were used as temporary morgues whenever local deaths occurred. After an inquest the bodies were taken to the parish church via an underground passage for church interment.

Often weeping can be heard coming from these blocked-off passages along with black shapes moving along the corridors of the pub. A poltergeist has an annoying habit of moving the barrels about in the cellar at night-much to the chagrin of the cellar man, I would think.

MARQUIS OF GRANBY

He was John Manners, leader of the Horse Grenadiers during the Seven Years War. To any officer or wounded soldier that had served under him, who would open a tavern named after him, he gave them £200; a contributory cause of the £37,000 of debts he left at his death.

The first sign is said to have been hung out at Hounslow by one Sumpter, a discharged trooper of the regiment of the guards which the Marquis had commanded as a colonel about 1760.

It is the grandson of the ninth earl whose bald-headed likeness is suspended from many inn signs; this was John Manners, 1721-70, eldest son of John, third Duke of Rutland, a brilliant cavalry leader who took part in the Seven Years War and also fought at Minden in 1759. As Colonel of the Blues, he led a cavalry charge at the battle of Warburg, 1760, and in the turmoil his wig blew off. As he galloped on, his men followed his bald pate and he so inspired them they afterwards boasted how the Marquis had 'gone for the enemy bald-headed', an expression ever since meaning to undertake an enterprise with vigour.

Colchester, Essex. Built circa 1520, although largely restored in 1914; it is now a Grade II* listed building.

In 1753 it was called the Crown; later. by 1769, the name had changed to Marquis of Granby. It is now called Ye Olds Marquis, with a hanging sign showing a portrait of the Marquis.

There is a story that the pub is haunted by James Parnell, a Quaker who died in 1656. He was charged with blasphemy after preaching at a Colchester church. First he was imprisoned at an inn which was on the same site as the present Marquis, before subsequently being held in Colchester Castle, where he was forced to climb a rope to reach his food. One day he fell to his death.

MALTINGS (THE)

A malting is where the grain is laid out on the floor, then wetted and continually turned until it just begins to sprout when growth is stopped by heating; this is when the sugar level is at its highest.

Ware, Hertfordshire. A two-storey whitewashed brick pub with a red-tiled roof and porch over the front door. The pub is a single L-shaped room, carpeted throughout and with a raised section on one side. Farmhouse pine furniture along with wood wall cladding finishes the description.

Until 2016 was known as the Worppell after the builder who constructed the building; before that the New Rose and Crown. It takes its modern name from Ware being a centre for malting during the eighteenth and nineteenth centuries, although there is no indication this was a malting.

Swinging sign shows three ears of wheat, white on a dark grey background.

MARROWBONE AND CLEAVER

It was the custom of butcher boys to 'serenade' newly married couples by beating a marrowbone against a cleaver, making a sound similar to a bell being rung. Largesse of a florin or half a crown was generally offered for this attention.

Formerly the band would consist of four cleavers, sometimes eight, each of a different tone which created a sort of indifferent bell-ringing. When well performed, it was not unpleasant. The butchers of Clare Market had the reputation of being the best performers. The last public appearance of this popular music was thought to be at the marriage of King George III in 1761.

Kirmington, Lincolnshire. Originally three cottages: one was lived in, one became a butcher's shop and the third a one-roomed pub. When the butcher retired, the pub took over his shop together with the remaining cottage.

The pub retains a two room system; with both rooms having an open fire and traditional furniture.

The sign shows a dog running off with a marrowbone followed by the butcher wielding his cleaver.

MARTIN'S ARMS

Colston Bassett, Nottinghamshire. A Grade II listed building of two-storey with a lean-to extension on one end. There is a single dormer window in the centre of the slate roof. The pub is rendered and whitewashed, covered in creeper along with a porch entrance to one side.

The windows are rather startling, as there are three tall eight-paned panels making a single large window with only the centre frame opening.

There is some confusion over the date when it was built; one reference gives a date of it being turned into an alehouse during 1690 by a farming family. However, a further story tells that the ale house was reputed to be the place where a Royalist plot was hatched to kill all of the occupants of Owthorpe Hall, which was owned by an officer in the Parliamentarian forces during the English Civil War, which indicates it was open prior to 1649. A further one tells it was built in the early nineteenth century – but this may mean that it was rebuilt at that time.

Inside it has two rooms, one of which is used for dining. It has an open fire and is decorated with a multitude of pictures above the high dado rail; here you are seated at highly polished dining room tables and chairs.

The other has a magnificent carved wooden Jacobean fire surround that came from the billiard room of nearby Colston Bassett Hall.

There are conflicting reports on how the pub got its name; one story says that the farming family who turned it into an ale house were named Martin. However, another source tells that it takes its name from the local squire, Mr Henry Martin, MP for Kinsale in County Cork, who sold the estate in 1864. So take yer pick!

There is no swinging sign, but there is a large wooden board on a gable end proclaiming the name.

MAYBUSH

Great Oakley, Essex. Another name for Hawthorne. First record of the pub was in 1769 when it appeared on the Alehouse Recognizance's with the licensee being John Winney. Haunted by an East Asian girl. In February 2016 it reopened as a cooperative run by the local community.

MAYPOLE

A maypole was generally set up for Mayday; it was a tall wooden pole erected in a number of European countries around which a dance was performed. The custom is thought to go back to pagan times, when, in some parts of Europe, the pole was a representation of the sacred trees such as Thors Oak. In Norse mythology it was possibly meant to be Yggdrasil – the world tree.

Other countries view it as a phallic symbol or a communal symbol; whatever the reason, usually the dance is performed by an equal number of boys and girls standing alternately and each holding a ribbon attached to the top of the pole. The boys dance round the pole one way and the girls in the opposite direction, weaving in and out of each other until the woven ribbons are used up and the children meet at the base of the maypole.

Cambridge, Cambridgeshire. This house was originally two pubs; the Maypole in Portugal Place and the Plume of Feathers in Park Street.

The rear patio contains a double helix to commemorate Francis Crick, who lived next door to the pub; he and James Watson worked out the structure of DNA. Along with this, a mural depicting a rural scene with maypoles is at the front of the pub.

A swinging sign shows people dancing round a maypole with striped awnings in the background.

MECHANICS ARMS

Nottingham, Nottinghamshire. It was first licensed in 1866 as a beer house. The building is a two-storey corner pub with a curved frontage on the apex of the corner. The building is a rare survivor of the clearances of the 1970s, when much of the area was flattened for redevelopment.

The pub is also known as the Pride of Erin, as it is an Irish-themed pub; it has no swinging sign.

At present the pub's future is uncertain as it is up for auction and may be sold for conversion into flats.

MERRY MONARCH

This was the soubriquet of Charles II, as was Old Rowley, the name taken from his favourite stallion. Some signs show him mounted on Old Rowley; others show a head-and-shoulders portrait. A very few show the painting by John Michael Wright.

Leicester, Leicestershire. Built in 1966, this is a two-storey brick estate pub on the end of a row of shops. A rectangular building with a flat roof and a single-storey wing on one end. It has a large bar with wood flooring and high ceilings; also has a function room.

Outside is a beer garden, and the swinging sign shows a copy of the painting of King Charles II in Garter Regalia by John Michael Wright.

MILL

Sudbury, Suffolk. Is a hotel, part of which has a weather-boarded façade painted white, standing on the banks of the River Stour. The building was originally a sixteenth century mill used for grinding corn.

There is a very scary story attached to the building; during the conversion to a hotel in 1977, a mummified cat was found in the roof, where it had been walled up when the hotel was built. It was widely believed at the time the presence of this animal would protect the structure from fire and bad luck.

The cat was taken to a nearby studio while renovations were made; however, shortly after a fire at the hotel caused much damage. Financial worries then halted work, followed by the studio in which the cat had been transferred catching fire.

The cat was quickly returned to the hotel.

Repairs in 1999 meant its removal again. During one fortnight, the road outside collapsed, the manager's office was flooded more than once and the person who removed the cat suffered an accident; once the relic was returned, things became something like normal… Coincidence? Maybe. You decide.

The mummified cat can be seen today through a glass panel in the floor in reception.

MINDEN ROSE

Bury St Edmunds, Suffolk. A modern two-storey brick-built estate pub. The sign showed a rose on either side of a redcoat. The name commemorates men of the 12th Foot, later to be the Suffolk Regiment, who fought at the battle of Minden in 1759. As the men advanced, they passed through some German gardens, where they picked roses to wear them in their caps. This event is still commemorated by the Minden regiments on 1st August, the anniversary of the battle, when roses are once more worn in their caps.

The pub is now closed and has been turned into a nursery.

MISCHIEF (THE)

Norwich, Norfolk. A Grade II listed building. Initials of AT on one gable stand for Alexander Thurston, who was a grocer in the mid-sixteenth century who probably had the house built.

At my last visit the pub was very proud that it did not supply food, have quiz nights, nor does it have any games teams, although the facilities were there. The mantra of the management is to make the pub a welcoming place without the restrictions these would place on customers.

At one end of the bar is a corner of carved stone work showing part of an arch with a decorated spandrel, although it is not known if it is in the original position.

The swinging sign was knocked down by a swerving bus, so the owners held a competition in 2012 for a unique sign with a prize of £1,000. The winner came up with a triangle of ten acrobatic mice standing on each other's shoulders-he was inspired by the collective noun for mice being a mischief.

MITRE AND KEYS

Both are papal symbols: the mitre for the bishop, the keys of Heaven for St Peter.

Leicester, Leicestershire. This three-storey brick pub had its origins in 1560, although it has been altered many times since then, the latest possibly in the 1920s or '30s, when an Art Deco façade was added. One unusual feature was that the last bay of the building did not belong to the pub but was a newsagents. The original pub had separate entrances for the public and lounge bars, as was the fashion in those days.

It appeared to have no swinging sign, although there was a large wall-mounted picture that looks like a bishop wearing a mitre holding some keys.

The building was demolished in the late 1960s.

The reason for including this now-defunct pub is that it was the only one of that name and possibly has a story behind the name. I would hazard a tenuous reason for it; thirty years previous to its construction, Cardinal Wolsey was being escorted to London on a dubious charge of treason, when he fell ill. This concerned his escorts, so they stopped at Leicester, where Wolsey died. He was buried at Leicester Cathedral. Did some landlord name his pub out of sympathy of the maligned cardinal? We shall never know, but it's a nice thought all the same.

MOLETRAP

Stapleford Tawney, Essex. A two hundred-year-old pub of a single storey, rendered with dormer windows set in the tiled roof and a small porch entrance.

Inside the single bar has oak beams and an open fire with traditional furniture; it is carpeted, except in front of the bar, which has a wooden floor.

The décor is mostly old photographs and bric-a-brac, which gives the pub a comfortable 'Olde World' charm; it is also a 'Quiet' pub, so conversation is not drowned out by a blaring jukebox or musak.

Outside there is a large garden and plenty of seating in front of the pub with views over the Essex countryside.

It is the only pub called this in the world; it was named by a previous owner, who invented a particular type of moletrap that looks like one of those grabs seen on lorries for unloading building supplies.

The swinging sign shows the instrument – white on a burgundy background.

The pub closed in 2018 but talks are ongoing to see if it can become an asset to the community.

MONTAGU ARMS

Barnwell, Northamptonshire. Built in 1601, it is a long, low two-storey stone building with a slate roof – unusually the three first-floor windows are set half in the roof and half in the stonework. It was originally three cottages constructed for workmen who were building the nearby manor house.

Swinging sign shows the Montagu Arms in a quartered shield.

The castle and manor of Barnwell belonged to the Abbey of Ramsey in Huntingdonshire until the dissolution, when King Henry VIII in 1540 granted the castle and manor to Sir Henry Montagu, Chief Justice to the King's Bench. The estate was later bought by the Prince Henry, Duke of Gloucester, who still retains it.

MOTHER REDCAP (OLD MOTHER REDCAP)

There are several ladies who claim this title dating from Elizabethan times, its origin being the red bonnet worn as part of an eccentric dress.

Often she was a witch in league with the devil, so 'tis said, and when she turned up with him a disaster was round the corner. Legend tells that her spells could only be broken if she were encircled with a golden ring.

One Mother Redcap, who lived on Wallasea Island, Essex, may have been a real person. Said to be a witch, she lived at a farm known as the Devil's House, where her familiar haunted a particular room, its presence made known by heavy wing beats near the ceiling in an unbearably cold temperature.

The title was also attributed to Moll Cutpurse, circa 1585-1660, a woman criminal of several aliases and masculine vigour, real name believed to be Mary Frith, who often dressed as a man and once did public penance for this. She was a notorious thief, known to have attacked General Fairfax on Hounslow Heath, for which she was sent to Newgate. She escaped from there by the use of bribery before finally dying of dropsy.

Mother Redcap was also the name given to an old nurse at Hungerford, Berkshire, famous for her longevity.

John Skelton, the English satirist, circa 1460-1529, and poet laureate to Henry VIII, says in a pamphlet she is the personification of Ellinor Rumming, the alewife, about whom he wrote verses; 'The Tunning of Elinour [sic] Rumming/Rummynge' – all spellings vary.

A poem that often went with the name is:

> Old Mother Redcap, according to her tale,
> Lived twenty and a hundred years by drinking good ale,
> It was her meat, it was her drink and medicine beside,
> And if she still had drank this ale she never would have died.

A further story told the original Mother Redcap was a follower of Marlborough's army in the reign of Queen Anne during the early eighteenth century. However, this idea is negated due to the existence of a token, dated 1667, mentioning in its inscription 'Mother Read Cap's [sic] in Holl[o]way'. Pubs and other businesses in those days often issued their own tokens in lieu of coins of the realm and were legal tender.

After all that, it may just have been a genetic term for any ale wife. So yer pays yer money and takes yer choice.

Luton, Bedfordshire. Sign shows an old woman in a shawl wearing a red leather cap pulling a pint of beer with her cat on the counter.

MUNTJAC

A small South-east Asian deer with a doglike bark and small tusks which has colonised parts of Bedfordshire after being imported into the country by the Duke of Bedford around 1900. They are now regarded as a pest.

Harrold, Bedfordshire. A two-storey seventeenth century stone building with a slate roof, although another history tells that it was first licensed in 1845. Inside is a long bar room with two fireplaces and a beamed ceiling. The restaurant at the rear has a stone surround inglenook fireplace and a covered well in the floor, which one source tells that when lit you can observe fish swimming in the clear water below.

The name was changed from the Globe in 2003 after a refurbishment. The swinging sign is gold lettering on a royal blue background.

It is the only pub of this name in the United Kingdom.

MUSGRAVE ARMS

Shillington, Bedfordshire. It was a beer house from at least 1847, when it was called the Royal Oak, until it gained a full licence sometime after 1862.

The swinging sign shows the arms of the Musgrave's which are an inverted triangle of six circles set in a shield surrounded by acanthus leaves and surmounted by a closed knight's helmet.

The name is taken from the Lords of the Manor of Aspley Bury which encompassed Shillington village.

Be not forgetful to entertain strangers –
for thereby some have entertained angels.

Sign over the door of the Crown Tavern, Clerkenwell.

NAG'S HEAD

Horses could be hired from some country inns and taverns, as travellers often had to change horses on a lengthy trip. This facility was advertised with appropriate signs: one of which could be a horse's head.

The word nag comes from Middle English, meaning a small horse suitable for riding, but is now used in a derogatory manner meaning an old, worn-out horse.

Enderby, Leicestershire. Here an annual Whit Monday ceremony, 'The Selling of the Wether', the hay crop or keep from a field called the Wether, was auctioned for the coming year. A silver coin was passed from hand to hand during the auction, only the person holding it was allowed to bid. The sale closed when the coin had made three circuits without an increased bid. The proceeds of the auction paid for a celebration dinner at the Nag's Head. John of Gaunt is said to have started the custom in the 1390s by giving each man a ewe, a wether (a male sheep) and a parcel of land in the parish of Enderby, he was always toasted during this ceremony. Due to the Wether being declared common land by the council in 1976, it could no longer be 'sold' in this way, which brought about the demise of the custom. Another piece of our heritage sold down the river by bureaucratic nonsense!

NARBOROUGH ARMS

Narborough, Leicestershire. Four hundred-year-old black-and-white inn. Once was a church or a monastery which is haunted by a monk dressed in a long black habit, who dissolves into a white mist which then disappears through a wall. A second apparition is wrapped in a shroud, although sightings of this one are quite rare.

NELSON (LORD)

Nelson was born in 1758 at the rectory at Burnham Thorpe in Norfolk, where his father was vicar; he was the sixth of eleven children. He joined the navy in 1771 as a seaman on a ship commanded by a maternal uncle. After various postings and bouts of malaria, he was given command of HMS *Badger*, in which he patrolled the Caribbean. Another bout of malaria had him sent home to England, where he fretted for another command.

In March 1777, after being given a further command and being once more sent to the Caribbean, he met and married Francis Nesbit, a widow living on Nevis.

In 1798 he destroyed the French fleet at the Battle of the Nile. It was during the battle of Copenhagen that he raised his telescope to his blind eye when ordered to break off the engagement. During his Mediterranean tour he met Emma Hamilton, who would become his mistress and mother of his daughter Horatia.

The year 1815 brought about his most famous battle; the Battle of Trafalgar. For Nelson it was his last battle, as he was shot by a French marksman. His body was transported back to England in a barrel of rum, where he was buried in St Paul's Cathedral.

Burnham Thorpe, Norfolk. A two-storey cottage-style pub that was built sometime around 1636. It was originally called the Plough but renamed after Nelson's victory at the Battle of the Nile (also called Battle of Aboukir Bay), where he fought and defeated the French fleet. The pub claims that it was the first to change its name to the local hero.

There is no bar as such; all drinks are served through a hatch in the tap room, beer being served straight from the barrel.

The pub has two drinks for which it is famous. Naturally they are both rum based; one contains a full-bloodied rum, called Nelson's Blood; the other is milder and spiced, as fit for a lady, called naturally enough, Lady Hamilton's Nip.

Story has it that on declaration of war against France, when he was given command of the *Agamemnon*, he celebrated here by entertaining the whole village to a final meal upstairs – except for those thought too young. When teased about this, one boy reacted by fighting those who laughed at him. Nelson called him a 'valiant young fellow', so his parents had him re-christened Valiant in the local church.

The swinging sign shows Nelson in his best uniform with all his awards pinned on his chest.

NELSON ARMS

Yarmouth, Norfolk. Story has it that when the fleet was standing off at Yarmouth Roads, a former landlord wished to interest custom from sailors of the fleet, so he sought permission from Admiral Nelson to call his house 'The Nelson Arms'. His Lordship gave full permission but reminded the landlord that his arms were only in the singular. The pub is now closed.

NEVER TURN BACK

Caister-on-Sea, Norfolk. A 1930s building almost on the beach. The entrance to both bars is by a common foyer set in an Art Deco tower, decorated with coloured stone and the name of the pub.

The pub takes its name from a tale that happened in November 1901. The Caister lifeboat was launched in a severe gale in order to aid a ship in trouble. The lifeboat was launched but was driven back towards the shore by the waves; it was launched again but was once more forced back to the shore, when it capsized, trapping the crew beneath the hull. Three were rescued, but nine crew members perished. At the inquest, James Haylett, the coxswain, was asked why the boat was launched in such adverse conditions; his reply was, "Caister men never turn back, sir!" For his part in rescuing his comrades he was awarded the RNLI Gold Medal.

The swinging sign is double-sided; one shows a hand about to grasp another one in the water; the other, the lifeboat plowing through the sea.

NEWCASTLE ARMS

Aspley, Nottinghamshire. Built in 1930 to a design by Evans, Clark and Wollatt. The building is a symmetrical two-storey double gable with central entrance, with the first-floor brick-faced whilst the ground floor is stone. Over the entrance in high relief is a shield and crest of the Dukes of Newcastle.

An unusual item – opposite the bar are two snob screens with a table and settle between them, making a small private area.

The pub takes its name from a local family who had lands in the area; it refers to the Duke of Newcastle-under-Lyme, not the town in Tyneside.

The swinging sign shows the coat of arms of the family with the motto 'loyaulte n'a honte' ('loyalty feels no shame').

NEW FAIRLOP OAK

Barkingside, Essex. Daniel Day was born into a wealthy brewing family in 1683. On the first Friday of July he would walk from Wapping to the Fairlop Oak in the forest – an agreed meeting place – where his tenants handed over their rents. He allowed then to pitch stalls round the oak to do a bit of trading while they waited. To encourage the mood of fraternity, Day would provide several sacks of beans and plenty of bacon.

The rent gathering developed into Fairlop Fair, enjoyed until the oak blew down in 1820. Tradition has it Daniel Day was buried in 1767 in a coffin made from a fallen branch of the tree. At the time oak was very valuable, because its wood was used for many purposes as it was strong and very durable.

Most church roof beams are made from oak, as are many old houses which have wooden frames, almost exclusively made from oak.

The swinging sign shows a gold tree silhouette in an oval of royal blue which commemorates the new oak tree that was planted after the demise of the ancient one.

NEW INN

The name is often given to a pub when a new building was erected on the site of a former one. Paradoxically 'new' inns are often among the most ancient. Another source tells that during the reign of Queen Elizabeth I she complained of the lack of suitable inns for travellers to stay at (herself included) so commanded that more should be built. This coincided with a time of relative peace and prosperity, so travellers were plenty and people were willing to risk money.

St Neots, Huntingdonshire. Haunted by the Earl of Holland, who lodged here whilst being taken to London for execution during the English Civil War. He is a tall man dressed in a long, dark cloak, who either peers around before disappearing through a closed door; or is seen sitting at a table writing.

Stowe, Buckinghamshire. Built by the Temple family in 1717 as a place for rest and refreshment for those visiting Stowe. A small guide book, the first for a country house, was written by Benton Seeley, which was sold to travellers staying at the New Inn – a very early example of a place specifically built for estate visitors. The intended entrance for visitors to the Stowe Landscape Gardens was through Bell Gate which would give a stunning view across the Octagon Lake to Stowe House.

This eighteenth century building is a fine example of a posting inn of the time, which differed from an ordinary inn insomuch that it provided horses for a post chaise; however, the location made it unlikely to attract passing trade, it was probably intended more to service the visitors.

The inn's combination with a farmstead is unusual, but it retained a traditional farmhouse feel, with the kitchen having a flagstone floor, a milking parlour and brew house, along with the courtyard being cobbled. Access to the upper floors was by north and south stair towers, and below there were cellars.

Careful restoration by the National Trust show rooms as they originally were, fires are lit, with bread baked, with invoices from past guests on view, creating an atmosphere redolent of the former bustle of the eighteenth century. Scraps of original wallpaper and bawdy words scrawled on hidden tiles by past builders have also come to light. The New Inn and its routes to the gardens opened in the spring of 2012, with visitors entering via the Bell Gate. Ring the bell there and see the gate open, giving visitors their first glimpse of Stowe, the Big House, just as Lord Cobham would have wished.

NOEL ARMS

The Noel family, Earls of Gainsborough, were a prominent Staffordshire family in the Middle Ages. In 1548 Andrew Noel purchased the manor of

Brooke in Rutland; later his second son, Sir Andrew Noel, built a house at Brooke when he inherited it on his father's death. He also bought other lands in Rutland and Leicestershire.

Motto: *'Tout bien ou rien'* ('The whole good or nothing'). The crest is a buck at gaze (full-faced), attired (horned).

Melton Mowbray, Leicestershire. A two-storey corner pub with three dormers; the corner entrance door has decorated pilasters supporting a portico and pediment, giving it a regal air. Inside is a quite large single room with some wall panelling and bare brickwork round the open fire. An unusual hexagonal stone graces the floor, while the ceiling has beams.

Outside is a small courtyard at the rear.

The swinging sign shows the family coat of arms.

NORMAN KING

Later called The Norman.

Dunstable, Bedfordshire. Reputed to be one of the oldest inns in England, the site dates back to 1109, when King Henry I was on the throne. The building has had a chequered life, having at some time being a museum, a dwelling house, a stable and a barn. It is thought to stand close to the site of 'Kingsbury', a once-royal palace for Henry I, who used it as a base when hunting the lands nearby.

The building was thatched with a plethora of oak beams and panelled walls with copper and brass fittings.

Since I last visited the building has been subjected to an arson attack in 2010 and at the time of writing is still a pile of ash.

Dunstable was at one time an important town which had a priory and was a royal borough during the time of Henry I. The town grew because it was the crossing point of the Icknield Way and Watling Street – two main Roman roads.

The building is now demolished. A sad end to such an historic building.

NUTSHELL

The Traverse, Bury St Edmunds, Suffolk. This is another contender for the smallest pub in England, the bar is only fifteen feet by seven feet, though the pub is built on three floors and measurements relate only to the ground floor, which is where the bar is. During March 1984, while a local radio station reported the event, 102 people and a dog managed to cram themselves into it.

The earliest record of the building is in 1844, when a fruitier, Peter Peck, sold it to another fruitier, Richard Carey. Sometime around 1867, part of the building was converted into a beer house. Six years later the building changed hands again – this time to the Stebbing family, who continued selling beer from the premises; they also had other business interests in the Traverse, including being fruitiers and pawnbrokers. The pub was billed as a Museum of Art and Curiosities, offering items carved from ivory, cardboard, ancient musical instruments and items carved from cork.

There is a huge collection of miniature curios which now include a ceiling covered with bank notes, a juke-box, a tiny snooker table and dartboard, and, somewhere, a mummified cat and mouse, along with a three-legged chicken. The cat is purported to keep witches away. It's amazing just how much memorabilia can be crammed into such a small space and still leave room for the customers!

The pub is also haunted by a small boy, who was reputedly murdered in one of the bedrooms, although he manifests himself mainly in the bar. A phantom monk wearing a long black habit and a large wooden cross also appears, as does the smell of a woman's perfume even when no one present is wearing any.

The sign depicts two blue tits feeding from a coconut shell.

> May the roof we sit ander ne'er fall in;
> May the friends agin us ne'er fall out.

Painted on the wall of the bar of The Tam O' Shanter, Ayr.

OAKLEY ARMS

Harrold, Bedfordshire. A sixteenth or seventeenth century two-storey limestone building with a slate roof. Formerly called the Blacksmiths' Arms.

John Noble, a brazier, and Thomas Noble, a tin, iron and zinc plate worker, were both recorded as being beer sellers in 1864; the name Blacksmiths' Arms may have been suggestive of their trades.

A Richard Wright was a tenant in 1890.

The Sharnbrook Petty Sessions Licensing Regulations, which began about 1901, has the Blacksmiths' Arms Beer house crossed through and the name replaced by the Oakley Arms. This change of name is odd, as Oakley is another village a few miles away and it seems doubtful if a new landlord would alter the name to another village, as that would almost certainly upset his present customers.

In 1927 the county valuer visiting the pub wrote that the building was owned by a Bedford brewer, with Dan Orpin as tenant. It comprised of two small bars, a cellar, a tap room and a private room. Outside was a brew house, a workshop, a stable, a cart shed and fowl houses, all put to good use.

To show how things have changed; the rent then was £12 per year and trade a barrel and a half, plus six to eight dozen bottles per week; this was when it was still a beer house. It seems to have become an inn between 1936 and 1940, still being listed as the Oakley Arms.

The modern pub has shrunk the number of rooms; there are now only two; a bar and a large lounge used for dining. However, Dan Orpin is still there, in spirit if not in body; his ghost is often seen sitting in the bar with a pint puffing on his pipe. Up until the 1960s the pub was still called 'Dan's place'.

The swinging sign shows what appears to be the Oakley family arms. although I can find no record of such a family in the area.

OLD ANGEL

Nottingham, Nottinghamshire. There has been a public house called the Angel in the Lace Market area since around 1676. The present building dates from circa 1800 and was originally two houses. During Queen Victoria's reign, a local lace maker, afraid his workers were not getting enough religious education, installed a chapel on the first floor which has since been turned into a gig area.

The religious connection does not stop there; deep below the cellars are some caves hewn out of the ground to form a crucifix, where it seems church services were held at one time. Not only has it been a church but also a brothel, although probably not at the same time.

The pub is a three-storey Grade II listed corner building with a stucco finish.

Two murders have been witnessed by the pub; one of a policeman, the other of a young prostitute who, it is said, still haunts the place.

OLD BELL AND STEELYARD.

Woodbridge, Suffolk. A building constructed circa 1549 as a terrace of cottages.

The pub over the years has had a variety of names, being called, the Bluebell, The Fox, Stilyards (an old spelling of steelyard). The Bell and the Three Goats; when it settled on the name Old Bell and Steelyard is uncertain, although the Steelyard was added circa 1600.

The steelyard was a simple weighing machine used to determine the load on wagons, which had been getting heavier and damaging the roads – if they were over two and a half tons, a toll had to be paid. The wagon was weighted before and after loading, while in all probability the drivers whetted their whistle. It was the original form of weighbridge.

Although it is certain the steelyard was affixed to the building at the date stated, when the building became a pub is less certain. One reference states between 1827 and 1841, while another plumbs for mid-seventeen century.

In 2018 the building was damaged when an HGV hit it; luckily the pub is back in business.

OLD BULLS HEAD

Broughton Astley, Leicestershire. Stands on the site of a previous pub. This pub has a most unusual ghost in a Victorian policeman!

In days gone by it was common practice for the police to visit pubs on a regular basis to ensure no laws were being broken. Our ghost appears to be about to enter the pub but disappears before he gets there.

Ware, Hertfordshire. Thought to have been built in the sixteenth century as a coaching house, although it was first mentioned in its present position in 1744 (this may have been caused by a change of road name or an alteration of the road's position). The two-storey part-timbered inn is the only surviving coaching house left in the town. Ware at one time was an important stopping place for the coaches, probably the penultimate stop before central London. The building is Grade II listed.

The open-plan room has oak beams and an inglenook fireplace with wood-moulded surround and set in a panelled wall.

The pub does have its ghosts; one is a tax collector who called at the premises but ended up being murdered there. I was not told how, but the reason can be guessed, as they have never been the most popular of people!

OLD COACH HOUSE

Ashby St Ledgers, Northamptonshire. The estate has had a chequered time from when it was given to Hugh de Grentemaisnil shortly after the Norman conquest. It passed through the Catesby family, who were involved with the Gunpowder Plot, then through several other owners until 1903, when the estate was bought by Viscount Wimborne. He employed Edwin Lutyens to redesign the house and village, which meant the village pub was demolished to make room for cottages. A former farmhouse on the estate was converted into a pub and named the Old Coach House.

The swinging sign shows a coach and horses.

OLD ENGLISH GENTLEMAN

A prototype phrase for the true patriot in the best sense of the word. It was not meant to be anyone in particular, in the same vein as John Bull or Uncle Sam.

There is a song from the early 1700s entitled 'A Fine Old English Gentleman' which might have inspired the name.

Charles Dickens also wrote a parody of 'A Fine Old English Gentleman' in 1841 after the Tories had taken over the government in a parliamentary election. It was printed in the Liberal journal *The Examiner.*

Saffron Walden, Essex. Nineteenth-century two-storey red-brick building with a tiled roof. The façade has an almost Dickensien look, with three tall eight-paned windows on either side of the entrance.

The décor has a collection of pictures of famous men, ranging from Oscar Wilde to the Duke of Wellington, many of which have a brief history of them attached.

At the front is a swinging sign showing the head and shoulders of an eighteenth century dandy holding his single-lens glass, and a buckle in his flowerpot hat. On the end of the building is a silhouette of the head of a gentleman.

OLD FERRY

Horning, Norfolk. Properly the Ferry Inn. A ferry still ran from here until the late 1960s, when it was discontinued, thereby ending a service which originated in Roman times. Situated beside the river Bure, there was a fifteenth century building here which was constructed as a mead store for the nearby St Benet's Abbey. Later, a large wherry hut, then used as a trading station on the Bure prior to WWI. It was later turned into the inn when holidays on the Broads were becoming popular. An oil painting in the bar reminds people what it looked like, as a direct hit from a German bomb in 1941 demolished this old building and a brass plate states 'Bombed 26th April, rebuilt 1955/6, presented to the Horning Ferry by No 141 Squadron Royal Air Force'.

Two gargoyles carved in black wood in the public bar came from the original inn.

A ghost is reported to appear at twenty-year intervals. It was while the inn was still the mead house that several monks, having taken mead tasting beyond its normal limits, saw a young girl passing along the river bank and dragged her into the mead house, where their vows of chastity were brutally forgotten. Realising too late what they had done, they pushed her lifeless body into the Bure. A girl in a grey-green cloak haunts the inn and glides into the bar to walk through the closed main door. One publican followed to see the wraith disappearing at the water's edge, close by where the ferry was moored.

OLD FERRY BOAT

Holywell, Cambridgeshire. Sometime called the Ye Olde Ferry Boat.

The bar has oak beams with a brick inglenook and wooden floors. On one beam is written 'in memory of Juliet Tewsley who died 17th March 1050 ad'.

One of the oldest inns in the country, with some saying it is the oldest. A building here can be dated to at least 1068 with a disputed history that stretches back to the sixth century. Hereward the Wake had frequently used the ferry here and there is a tradition he crossed the Ouse to this inn when escaping from the Normans.

Men can still recall helping to work the ferry, which saved farmers at least eight miles of droving when taking animals to market.

The inn is reputedly haunted, particularly on the night of 17th March, by the ghost of Juliette Tewsley or Tousely, a young girl who hanged herself on that date in 1050 from a willow by the Ouse when she was rejected by Tom Zoul or Thomas Roul, a local woodcutter. It has become known as Juliette's Eve. Her grave was marked by a simple slab of grey stone in unconsecrated ground near where she died. Later the inn was enlarged over the grave and the gravestone can be seen in the floor of the bar.

There are reports of odd happenings – strange sounds, the opening and closing of doors, and the experience of a locked door unaccountably unfastened. Dogs do not like the bar, often growling when close to the slab. On occasions music, described as old-fashioned and beautiful, seems to come from nowhere, which, strangely, can only be heard by women.

On the anniversary of her death, St Patrick's Day, people gather at the inn hoping to see her ghost rise from the grave at midnight and drift towards the river bank. It is recorded the inn obtained special licence to stay open until the witching hour of midnight on this date in anticipation of a sighting, but the last person who claimed to have seen anything died in the 1960s.

(YE) OLD FOUR SWANS

Waltham Cross, Essex. A very old inn that was an important coaching house; it claimed on the sign to date from 1260, which would date it thirty years before King Edward I had the 'Eleanor Crosses' built, so it is possible that this may have been one of the places where the men escorting the body boarded.

Waltham Cross was, until the coming of the railway, only ever a hamlet, even though it was a major route in and out of London for East Anglia. In 1811 there were only one hundred houses in the hamlet.

The last building on the site was constructed in the early seventeenth century; even then it had been altered considerably by the time the site was redeveloped in the 1960s.

It had a sign of four swans on a beam stretching across the very busy road; story has it the sign was erected by Royal Charter and could only be removed by an Act of Parliament. Which brings another tale to mind; it was reported that locals defended the sign when the tram company wanted to destroy it so they could continue their tramway. It seems they may have been unsuccessful, as the sign was still erected in 1950.

Power to the people!

OLD GARRISON

Southend-on-Sea, Essex. Built in 1898 (another source says 1856) as a medical centre for the troops, and their families stationed at Shoeburyness Army Barracks across the road.

Called the Captain Mannering from 1984, this was supposed to be the name of the character in 'Dad's Army' but the sign writer failed to spell the name Mainwaring correctly. Later called the Garrison Arms until a refurbishment in 2012.

The pub is haunted by the sound of children playing in the bar, but when the door is opened there is no one to be seen. Also a man in a white orderly's coat is sometimes seen in the bar area.

OLD NICK'S TAVERN

Horncastle, Lincolnshire. Built in 1752 as a coaching house, this is one of the only original buildings left in the town.

Has as a sign showing a clever stylistic, depiction of the devil in black on a red background. His Satanic Majesty is merely a few fluent lines which somehow conveys a sinuous menace.

OLD PACKHORSE

Kensworth, Bedfordshire. This pub could possibly have been built on or near the site of a much earlier place of rest where travellers could get food and drink, as it is on the Watling Street – an ancient Roman road.

The name would have been taken from the horses that carried goods in panniers around the country.

A suicidal ghost (if there can be such a thing) haunts the front of the pub; he has a habit of stepping out in front of passing cars. He is said to be six feet tall and wearing white clothing.

OLDE PARISH OVEN

Thorpe Salvin, Nottinghamshire. Built in 1972 on the site of a farmhouse that had the village oven, which once served the whole parish, the original oven door being built into the bar fireplace. A parish oven was usually the local baker, who, when he had finished baking, would allow parishioners to cook their own pastry's or perhaps, on odd occasions, a joint of meat, as few if any would have had their own oven – nearly all cooking being done over an open fire.

The swinging sign shows a man and a woman at the oven with cooked goodies on the table.

In Bedfordshire, and probably elsewhere, to have a mouth like a parish oven was an insult handed out to someone who gossiped or talked too much.

The only pub with this name in the United Kingdom.

OLD RAMME

Mansfield, Nottinghamshire. Believed to be sixteenth century, the pub is a two-storey half-timbered in the form of an L. The buildings on either side being constructed at a different distance from the road gives the footpath a dog leg which the pub fills with a small single-storey extension.

It is reputedly haunted by two monks who were supposed to have been crushed in a rock fall in the tunnel that connected the pub with nearby priory.

The swinging sign shows a ram in all his glory, perhaps indicating the pub had something to do with the wool trade. As there was a priory nearby, perhaps it was a place where wool merchants gathered before their goods were weighted by the monks.

OLD SUN INN

Ampthill, Bedfordshire. Built in 1766 originally as two cottages which later became the pub. Set back from the road, close to the town centre, with two bars and a games room. One room is decorated with photos of old Ampthill researched by a landlord.

The pub was at one time owned by an Ampthill brewer called Monks & Co. who then sold it in 1926 to the Luton brewer JWGreen; they in turn were merged with Flowers brewery, who were then acquired by the giant Whitbread.

The sign has a sun face with wavy rays.

OLD SWAN

The sign is usually what else but a…

Woughton on the Green, Buckinghamshire. A two-storey, black-and-white, L-shaped half-timbered and brick building from circa 1730, making it one of the oldest buildings in the area.

The pub had a recent refurbishment, but many features remain. With a crooked roof and low ceilings, along with many exposed beams, the open plan is broken up by having different levels.

Swinging sign shows a stylised white swan on a dark grey background.

A gloomy and unlighted room in the centre of the building was once known as the Prison Room, where those travelling on Their Majesty's pleasure were confined for the night. Conversely there are also tales of wanted men being hidden there by the landlord until the heat was off.

During the eighteenth century Dick Turpin reputedly used this inn as a base between robberies, as the Old Watling Street runs nearby, which would have provided good hunting for him and his gang.

Story has it that he stopped at the inn when being pursued and quickly re-shod his horse with horseshoes pointing backwards. The pursuers rode off in the opposite direction. A good story for the publican to tell on a night when the pub was full!

Ghosts of Turpin and his horse have often been seen in the district at night. One wonders if he still haunts and, if so, where, as this village has been swallowed up and is now part of Milton Keynes.

Another ghost spoken of by locals at the inn was Old Curley, who, with his dog, was said to come out of Curley Bush beyond the crossroads on which the pub stands. Today such tales are treated lightly, but to the older generation he was a grim reality – though, as one local put it, "They allus 'spec to see 'im an' their fright done the rest."

OLIVER CROMWELL

Cromwell was born into a middle gentry family at Huntingdon on 25th April, 1599. The family was a descendent from Thomas Cromwell, King Henry VIII's chief minister who had acquired lands from the monasteries during the dissolution of the church under Henry.

Cromwell was a staunch Puritan who made life for both Catholic and Protestants uncomfortable, as well as having many pub names changed, especially any that had religious connotations.

He was elected as Member of Parliament for Huntingdon in 1628 then later for Cambridge.

In 1642 he took the Parliamentarian side at the beginning of the English Civil War, before quickly becoming Lieutenant General in the army, then shortly after, second in command. Cromwell instigated a number of new ideas, one of which was the New Model Army, which became known as roundheads due to the helmets they wore.

In December 1648 he was one of fifty-nine members who signed King Charles I's death warrant, followed by the King's execution the following month.

An inn named 'Oliver Cromwell' would seem a tribute and would be frowned upon by the monarchy. However, one called 'Cromwell's Head' suggests jubilation, as his body was disinterred two years after its burial in Westminster Abbey during 1658 and hanged on the gallows at Tyburn, before it was later reburied.

In 1661, following his restoration to the throne, Charles II took revenge for his father's death and had the body of Oliver Cromwell disinterred, displaying his head at Westminster Hall, where it remained for twenty-four years as a grim reminder to those who opposed the monarchy.

St Ives, Cambridgeshire. The building was constructed as a cottage, until circa 1840, when it became a pub.

The most startling thing about this pub is the hanging sign; it is a massive ornate wrought-iron bracket that stretches out from the pub to the middle of the road. It shows a shield quartered that has the cross of St George in two of the quarters and a saltire of Scotland and the Harp of Ireland in the other two. It shows a portrait of Cromwell's head on one side with a castle on the other. In the centre of the shield is a smaller one with an English lion.

OPEN GATE

Ulceby, Lincolnshire. There are two white gates hung on the front of the building; one tells us; 'the gate hangs well and hinders none, refresh and pay and travel on'. The other states; 'call at the gate to taste the tap, drink and be merry but keep off the strap'.

The pub is now closed.

OPEN HEARTH

The name usually refers to an early method of steelmaking and is present mostly in steel towns, although other interpretations of the name exist.

Corby, Northamptonshire. A two-storey brick building constructed in the late 1940s whose name commemorated Corby's heritage as a major steel making town. Sadly the steel works closed, as did the pub in 2014, which is awaiting it fate – at the time of writing there is a planning application to convert it into flats.

Scunthorpe, Lincolnshire. Although the name reflects the town's heritage as a steel making town, the hanging sign shows two men sitting in front of an open fire, presumably in the pub.

ORANGE TREE

The orange tree was introduced into England by Sir Thomas Gresham in the late 1500s.Growing the trees was a Victorian fad and so became popular on inn signs. It could also be said to show allegiance to the Prince of Orange, later William III.

Hitchin, Hertfordshire. The pub was built in 1976, although there was formerly a pub on the site from 1902 or earlier.

Advertises a secret garden at the rear.

OSTRICH

Colnbrook, Buckinghamshire. It is said the village took its name from this, Cole-in-the-brook.

The original building on this site, created on the orders of Bishop Milo Crispin, dating from 1106, was initially a hospice belonging to Abingdon Abbey, which was formerly named the Crane. The present name is a corruption of hospice, which became Ospridge and then Ostrich.

King John is said to have stopped here for a tankard of ale on his way to Runnymede in 1215, as did Queen Elizabeth I and, who else but Dick Turpin. (you can't keep a good man down!).

The village grew up around coaching inns that abounded for travellers along the Great West Road from London to the West Country: in 1577, there were as many as ten inns listed here.

The timber-framed building dates as an inn from circa 1500. The host in the seventeenth century was one Jarman, with whom rich guests risked death at his hands. This landlord, wishing to rob them of their goods, had designed a bed – a replica of which can be seen today – and nailed it to the trapdoor above the kitchen. Prosperous guests would be shown to this Blue Room, and while they slept, the landlord and his wife would unbolt the trapdoor and guests would be hurled while asleep into a vat of boiling fat in the kitchen below. It is thought as many as sixty died at the inn. Bodies were then slung into the nearby river whilst the horses and luggage were sold.

Jarman was finally caught when the horse of one of the victims, a man named Cole, was found wandering, and a search led to the discovery of the man's body in a stream.

According to some accounts, 'Old Cole', as he seems to have been popularly known in the seventeenth century, may have been an original of the 'Old King Cole' of the nursery rhyme.

Ghosts of these unfortunates and others still continue to haunt the place.

Around the beginning of the twentieth century, the landlady of the Ostrich still showed the murder bedroom on request, although the falling trapdoor no longer existed.

Ipswich, Suffolk. The name of the pub is said to be taken from the coat of arms of Sir Edward Coke, 1552-1633, which featured an ostrich. He was lawyer and local lord of the manor who became speaker of the House of Commons. He also owned Holkham Hall in Norfolk.

Built circa 1610 close to Bourne Bridge in an area called Oyster Reach – which may have contributed to the name, as a Suffolk accent would surely sound both names similarly.

OUR MUTUAL FRIEND

Stevenage, Hertfordshire. Built in 1963, this two-storey red-brick modern estate pub has a contemporary-style roof made of neither slate nor tiles but some type of material. The main building has a single-storey extension at one end.

The lounge bar is trying to recreate the atmosphere of the Old Mutual pub, which was demolished in the 1960s to make way for the 'New Town' and which this pub replaces.

Charles Dickens's novel of this name appeared in weekly parts between 1864 and 1865.

I would give all my fame for a pot of ale.

Henry V.

PALMER ARMS

Dorney, Buckinghamshire. The village was mentioned in the Domesday Book; the name is said to be a derivation from the Saxon 'Island of Bees' and the village has been famous for its honey since then.

An old coaching inn and at one time the public house for the estate workers employed by the Palmer family, lords of the manor here for 450 years.

Although it has its roots back in the fifteenth century, it has only been a public house since the eighteenth century. It looks very much like a 1930s painted-brick building with a pair of bay windows on the ground floor joined by a flat roof.

In recent times has been refurbished in the style of a traditional country inn. A notice in the pub states. "[King] Charles II was presented with one of the first pineapples to be bought back from Barbados. After eating the fruit he gave the spiky top to Roger Palmer who brought it back to Dorney and planted it. The pineapple grew and eventually produced fruit – it was the first pineapple to be grown in Britain circa 1662. Palmer presented the fruit to the King".

A 'White Lady' (makes a change from the 'Grey Lady') haunts rooms upstairs, though she has not been seen lately.

The hanging sign shows the arms of the Palmer family with their motto *'Palmen Virtuti'* ('virtuous Palmer').

PEACOCK

A religious symbol referred to in Revelation 4:6:

'Before the throne there was a sea of glass, like crystal. And in the mist of the throne, and around the throne, were four living creatures with eyes in front and in back.'

The tail of the Peacock, with its thousand eyes are symbolic of omnipotence, often ascribed to the Archangel Michael. Also there is an ancient myth that the peacock's flesh did not decay, so it became a symbol of immortality.

A peacock is also seen as a symbol of resurrection, as when he sheds his tail the new ones are more brilliant than the ones he shed.

Chelsworth, Suffolk. Constructed in the fourteenth century, the building did not become a licensed premises until about 1855, although it may have been a beer house prior to that date. The original medieval use was thought to have been a hospice for pilgrims on their way to St Edmund's shrine at Bury.

It may have taken its name from a previous landlord (perhaps the first), whose wife's maiden name was Peacock. The pub also ran a shop at the front of the house until 1977, when it closed due to lack of support.

The swinging sign shows a peacock trailing his tail.

PELDON ROSE

Peldon, Essex. Situated on the edge of the Essex salt marshes, this is a fifteenth century inn that has altered little over the years. Although the building has been dated from the fifteenth century, it is thought parts may be much older, possibly from 1380, and as the pond was mentioned in the Domesday Book it is conceivably even older. Being close to the tidal causeway leading to Mersea Island, it would have been a natural stopping place for travellers when the road ahead was covered by the tide.

To one side of the pub is the aforementioned pond, much used as a smugglers' storehouse as it contains a deep well into which weighted barrels were lowered with ropes until the dreaded Revenue had gone.

The building was damaged in 1884 by an earthquake that was the severest ever to hit the United Kingdom, measuring 5.1 on the Richter scale.

One family, the Pullens ran the pub for over fifty years, taking it over some time around 1881, when George Pullen, who was also a market gardener, took over the running of the pub. The line continued until at least 1937.

The swinging sign is plain writing with a stylised rose in white on a purple red background.

Between the inn and the causeway, the ghost of a Roman centurion has been seen as recently as the 1970s.

PHEASANT

A sign every countryman would recognise and probably had eaten too, despite the gamekeepers' best efforts.

Brill, Buckinghamshire. A seventeenth century inn regularly frequented by Roald Dahl, who lived in nearby Great Missenden; he collected material here for his short stories by listening to local yarns. Another literary figure was JRR Tolkien, who reputedly based some of the places of the Shire in the *Lord of the Rings* on the area, even using one of the real names, Buckland.

The pub was refurbished in 2011, opening up the ceiling to show the exposed beams and the slate on the floor.

The village is also famous as being the hideout of the Great Train Robbers at Leatherslade Farm, which is in the village.

The swinging sign shows a cock pheasant in all his glory.

PICKEREL

Ixworth, Suffolk. The name in this instance is spelt in the medieval way of Pykkerel. A pickerel is a young pike in this case, although it can mean a dunlin.

Parts date from the sixteenth century, although much restored in the nineteenth century.

Advertised as a commercial and family inn, during the coaching era, on the road to Diss, and then onwards to Lowestoft and Norwich. Both the stable block at the rear and the main building are a Grade II listed building.

The pub is haunted by an old lady who watches people asleep from the end of their bed or walks around the pub.

The hanging sign shows the fish.

PIED PIPER

Scunthorpe, Lincolnshire. An estate pub built in the 1960s, when Scunthorpe was an emerging steel town.

In most pubs of this name, it commemorates the story of the Pied Piper of Hamelin in Germany, as told in the nineteenth century poem by Robert Browning.

Legend has it that in the thirteenth century a man dressed in pied clothes agreed to rid the town of an infestation of rats, which he did by playing his pipe, which the rats followed. He led them to the river, where all but one drowned. When he returned to the town in order to claim his one thousand guilders reward, the mayor and townsfolk refused to honour their agreement, trying to fob the piper off with fifty guilders.

As his revenge he piped again, only this time the children followed him, with the towns people unable to stop him. He led the children up a hill, where a magic cave opened up then swallowed them all.

This moralistic story concerning the rats did not appear until the sixteenth century; however, something did happen in Hamelin during June 1284, but what that was is not clear. At the same time parts of Transylvania had an influx of new people, who, legends tell, were led out from a cave in the mountains. To this day many have similar names as would be found in Hamelin. So did they emigrate from Hamelin or were they led? You guess.

The swinging sign shows the piper, followed by the rats.

PIG AND ABBOT

Abington Pigotts, Cambridgeshire. Built during the reign of Queen Anne.

In a separate dining room, which, at the time of writing, unusually used table cloths which looked very neat and, I may add, professional. (It is time other 'gastro pubs' started earning their money and giving the customer the service he is paying for; it's all part of the dining experience they like to harp on about.) Restored some time ago but retained the original doors and windows along with much of its old-world character. Saved from closure by a village buy-out in 1997. Was called the Darby and Joan from early eighteenth century until the 1980s, when it took on the present name, which is, in part, a pun on the village name.

The old sign shows an abbot holding a plate with a pig's head on it; the modern one is plain gold writing on a maroon background with a pig's and an abbot's head in pink.

PILGRIM'S PROGRESS

Bedford, Bedfordshire. A huge corner pub that belongs to a national chain. Inside the décor is well up to the standard of this chain, who remodelled the pub in 2016 to make two outside seating areas, along with a number inside, including first-floor seating.

Takes its name from the book by Bedfordshire's most famous son, John Bunyan, who was born in nearby Elstree.

The swinging sign is a half statue of Pilgrim, with his bags and hat.

PINK AND LILY INN

Lacey Green, Buckinghamshire. Eighteenth century two-storey painted brick with what looks like either another cottage on the end or an extension that that has been added at some time. One feature is unusual; the entrance porch; instead of entering as usual under the apex, with this one you go through the side. Possibly something to do with the prevailing wind – it's different.

Inside the Rupert Brooke room is kept much as it was during his time, with a carpet-covered tiled floor, high-back settles and a huge brick surround open fireplace that has a massive oak beam supporting the chimney breast. There is a second room of the bar that has soft furnishings around a further open fire with some tables for casual dining.

A separate dining room in the 'extension' down four steps, has wooden floors covered with a large carpet and lit by a lovely chandelier.

The swinging sign at one time had a painting of Rupert Brooke with the pub in the background, sadly that has gone, to be replaced with plain white lettering on a black background.

The story regarding this wonderful name is that it came about from a romantic encounter between Mr Pink, the butler, and Miss Lillie, a chambermaid – both of whom worked at nearby Hampden House, but later in about 1800, took over a private house which they turned it into a pub, and so named it.

Rupert Brooke's association with the pub came later, before WWI, when out walking in the Chiltern Hills he came across it then introduced it to some of his friends in the Bloomsbury Set, especially Jacques Raverat. The two of them often visited the inn and on one occasion immortalised it with a poem that starts;

Never came there to the Pink,
Two men as we, I think,
Never came there to the Lily,
Two men so rich and silly.

Photographs of him and the Bloomsbury Set, including Virginia Woolf, are scattered round the walls, and a copy of one of his poems is displayed over the old fireplace.

A wonderfully unique name.

PLEASURE BOAT

Hickling, Norfolk. This dates from at least 1856 and is situated on the northern shore of Hickling Broad – close enough to the water that if you're unsteady on your feet you should keep close to the building, or get wet!

A couple of notices caught my eye; one told 'be nice or leave', while another behind the bar read 'prices vary according to customer's attitude'. A pair of thoughts most landlords would echo.

The pub is approached by 'The Staithe', a local term for a quay or landing place, which is apt, as the pub has its own moorings.

PLOUGH

Emblem of abundance and fertility as well as denoting local agriculture. Many signs show the group of seven stars in Ursa Major, which look like an ancient plough.

Up until the end of the nineteenth century country people observed a custom called 'Plough Monday', which occurred on the first Monday after Epiphany. The custom involved a plough which was sometimes decorated, being dragged round the community by a group of men with blackened faces dressed in various daft costumes. They would accept food or drink in lieu of money; the money being used to pay for 'Plough Lights', candles that were kept burning in the church during the winter months. Later the plough would be blessed by the priest, but this also was frowned upon by the Puritans, who considered it a pagan ritual. In the middle of the twentieth century, I can vaguely remember going to a service at the village church where the plough was blessed – so perhaps the old custom has not died out completely!

Bolnhurst, Bedfordshire. Built in the fifteenth century, this was once a farm called Brayes on the edge of the village and believed to have been a checkpoint manned by Henry VIII's soldiers at the time his first wife, Catherine of Aragon, was imprisoned at Kimbolton Castle, where she died. Later it became the Plough and today forms part of the larger pub, Ye Olde Plough, which retains part of the original moat around the property.

It is whitewashed, with tiny windows, thick walls and mellow-pitched roof. The interior is low-beamed with great open fires and traditional décor, all very much in keeping with its age.

Great Munden, near Ware, Hertfordshire. In a specially built extension to the pub is a full-size working Compton theatre organ, which can be heard as well as seen.

Winchmore Hill, Buckinghamshire. It was here that two brothers were enjoying a pint, when they began talking about sweets they remembered as children. The idea came to them to enquire if many were still available and, if so, to market them. From this idea was born A Quarter Of. The shop, created on the web, has been so successful it now enjoys an international following, seeds of which venture were planted in the Plough.

PLUME OF FEATHERS

Refers to the of the Prince of Wales; a plume of three ostrich feathers, first adopted as a crest by Edward, the Black Prince, also known as the Fleur de Lys.

Welwyn, Upper Green, Hertfordshire. Constructed circa 1596. Originally built as a hunting lodge for Queen Elizabeth, some of the Elizabethan features remain, such as large open fires, flagstone floors, beams and a wooden bar. It later became the haunt of highwaymen and is said to have several ghosts, particularly an unknown lady in grey.

PRINCE RUPERT

Prince Rupert was born on 17th December, 1619, in Prague. His full title was Count Palatine of the Rhine, Duke of Bavaria, although better known as Prince Rupert of the Rhine. He was the third son of Elector Palatine Frederick V and Elizabeth, daughter of James I of Scotland and VI of England, and sister of King Charles I.

He became a soldier and fought in the Thirty Years War of 1618-1648. This gave him useful military experience which would stand him in good stead later when he was appointed as the leader of the Royalist cavalry during the English Civil War. He fought in several battles with mixed results until he advised the King to seek treaty with Parliament. When the King withdrew his commission, he left for exile in Holland.

When he was Commander in Chief of the Royalist fleet he was routed by Admiral Blake off Carthagena. Rupert escaped to the West Indies, returning later to Germany, where he lived till the Restoration.

He was the third founding member of the Royal Society, where he was known as the 'Philosophic Warrior'.

Newark, Nottinghamshire. The building is an example of a Wealdon House, dating from circa 1450; it is Grade II listed. A two-storey half-timbered pub with the ground floor being made of brick and the first-floor timbers of irregular shape due to age. One half is jettied whilst the other has a curiously curved wall into the eaves and the tiled roof.

Formerly called the Woolpack, which was an apt name as the town was at one time an important centre of the wool and cloth trade.

The swinging sign is plain lettering, white on green grey background.

PRINTER'S DEVIL

This name originated in the seventeenth century and was given to the errand boy or apprentice to the printing trade, who would mix the ink or fetch type, along with any other mundane task required of him. The appellation was due to the boys being unable to keep themselves entirely free from being smudged with the black ink so consequently looked like Satan. Another version tells that the name applies to the 'little devil' that alters the typeface to create misprints and generally messes up the printing procedure.

Slough, Buckinghamshire. Originally called the Bricklayers Arms to commemorate the local brickyards, the name was changed sometime in the 1960s, when the *Slough Observer* opened an office nearby.

This pub has closed, and as this was only one of three, which are all now closed the others being in London and Bristol it looks as though another unique name has gone for ever.

PRIORY

Dunstable, Bedfordshire. Built in 1973, then called the Chiltern, after the nearby hills; later the name was changed to the Priory, reflecting the ancient priory that was in the town. The pub is now closed and awaiting its fate.

Dunstable was a royal borough in the reign of Henry I, who ruled 1100-35; he granted a charter to the Augustinian priory he had built, as Dunstable was an important settlement, being at the crossing place of two ancient roads.

During excavations of the priory site in 1965, an enamelled white swan was found, made in circa 1400. What it was doing in the priory is something of a mystery, although it could have been left for safe keeping, especially if there was an anchorite there, as valuables were often left with such people.

PUNCH HOUSE

Horncastle, Lincolnshire. An arresting-looking public house built in the 1860s on the corner curve of a street, making the pub somewhat egg-shaped at one end. The sign is of three ancients sitting happily round a steaming punch bowl.

There is a notice on the front beside the door which asks patrons (and no doubt others) to leave the premises quietly and respect the neighbours. A rather nice touch, which I notice has been taken up by many others of late.

PYEWIPE

Fossebank, Lincoln. Named after the Lincolnshire dialect for the Lapwing, which gets its name from the Old English *'hleapewince'.* meaning to move sideways and leap. It is supposed to refer to the birds' erratic flight but it could equally refer to the habit of drawing a predator away from the nest by pretending to have a broken wing by jumping and dragging the wing along the ground.

Set in four acres of grounds, this is a canal-side inn with a beer garden and patio. It is beside the Roman-built Fossedyke navigational canal, so called, as the story goes, as when the Britons who had been forced to dig the canal had finished, the Romans gave then the privilege of naming it, so they called it 'Fossdyke', as it was the first dyke they had dug.

A patio overlooks the canal and has views over the Lincolnshire countryside and the cathedral.

> A man hath no better thing under the sun
> than to eat and drink and be merry.

The Bible.

QUEEN ELEANOR

Wootton, Northamptonshire. A large red-brick two-storey pub belonging to one of a national chain of eating pubs.

The pub takes its name from the nearby Eleanor Cross, one of only three to survive from the 1290s.

When Queen Eleanor of Castile died at Harby near Lincoln in 1290, her husband King Edward I decreed that in every place where the corpse rested there was to be built a cross 'of cunning workmanship' to be erected in memory of her. There were twelve crosses, one at each of the resting places made by her cortege on its way to Westminster Abbey in 1290.

The twelve stopping places are; Lincoln, Grantham, Stamford, GEDDINGTON, HARDINGSTONE, Stony Stratford, Woburn, Dunstable, St. Albans, WALTHAM CROSS, Cheapside in London, Charing, which then was a tiny village near Westminster where the cortege rested before moving on to Westminster Abbey. The three that survive are in capital letters.

Sadly many of the sites are unknown, as during the English Civil War the Puritans destroyed them, as they thought crosses were idolatry.

The cross in front of Charing Cross Station in the Strand is a Victorian copy; the old cross, made of Caen stone, was demolished in 1643, it stood at the top of Whitehall, where the statue of King Charles I now stands.

QUEEN OF HEARTS

This name was given to Lady Elizabeth Stuart, eldest daughter of James I of England, who married Frederick V, Elector of the Palatinate, chosen King of Bohemia in 1613. It was through her the family of Brunswick succeeded to the British throne.

Known for her amiable character and engaging manners, she was also called the Winter Queen, as her husband's reign only lasted one winter.

It is also one of the court cards in a pack of playing cards.

The modern pub in Daventry is dedicated to Princess Diana, who is buried a few miles away at Althorpe House.

The swinging sign is plain white lettering on a burgundy background.

Lenwade, Norfolk. Looks as though the building was originally several cottages that had a pantile roof, now rendered and painted.

Was a pub called the King of Hearts until 1982, when it became a tea shop. It was reopened in 2016 as the Queen of Hearts, again as a tea shop but this time also as a traditional bar and restaurant.

Inside is an open-plan room connected by arches.

The sign outside shows a red heart surrounded by gold acanthus leaves with the name inside a heart in white lettering, all on a red background.

QUEENS HEAD

Usually refers to Queen Victoria, with her head following that on the coinage of the time, which was called either Bun or Old. The bun was with her hair in a bun at the back and with a young face. The Old was exactly that; when she was dressed in mourning for Prince Albert – even though he had died some years earlier – the name stuck, and of course when she died she was often referred to as the Old Queen.

It may also have been Queen Elizabeth I or, I remember some years ago in London before the political correctness brigade had their claws into common sense, a head and shoulder of Quentin Crisp, who was a larger-than-life homosexual at the time and author of the book 'The Naked Civil Servant'.

A story regarding Elizabeth I goes that she had an official visit every pub that was called the Queens Head; if the picture on the sign was not a good representation of her ladyship it was taken down and burnt. Only those which were up to standard were allowed to remain. No doubt many were burned, as there were only a few people in the countryside who had ever seen the Queen, let alone paint her portrait!

Says a lot for royal vanity!

Harston, Cambridgeshire. The ghost of a White Lady has been seen walking from the inn to Mill Road. She has also been reported throwing herself into the river from the bridge on the road to Haslingfield.

Maldon, Essex. Situated on the quayside with a waterfront terrace. An annual mud race is run by the inn across the river at low tide in aid of local charities.

Newton, Cambridgeshire. Built as a farmhouse in 1680, it stands on the meeting of five roads on the former London to Cambridge coaching route and a major stopping place.

Devil among the Tailors, a version of table skittles, and Nine Men's Morris, an Elizabethan board game in some districts called Merrills or Merels and in others Marlipins, can be played here.

An inn popular with monarchs: George V and the German Kaiser drank here before hostilities of 1914, and the Shah of Persia (Iran) and his wife are known to have had lunch in the 1960s.

On the bar wall is a list of landlords since 1729.

Unusually Anne of Cleves is depicted on the sign, although there is no known connection.

A good wine should be drunk, not worshipped,
A landlady should be worshipped, not drunk!

Anon.

RANCLIFFE ARMS

The 1st Baron Rancliffe was Thomas Boothby Parkyns, the eldest son of Sir Thomas Parkyns. As an officer in the British Army he was equerry to Prince Henry, Duke of Cumberland, and at the same time elected as a Member of Parliament for Stocksbridge, then later Leicester, until his death in 1800.

Bunny, Nottinghamshire. A seventeenth-century coaching inn thought to have been built by Sir Thomas Parkyns, although it is possible there was a public house of sorts on the site from much earlier. He also built most of the village of Bunny to his own design

The inn became an important coaching inn when a new road from Nottingham to the south was opened. One story tells of all the customers going outside to watch Henry VII's troops marching past on their way to the Battle of Stoke in 1487.

This is a structure of two parts; the whole building is of two stories. The right-hand side facing the road has two gables and on the far right is the old arch for the coaches to enter. This is now a large window with an arched top. Between the gables on the ground floor is a small bay window and an entrance door.

At the left hand of the building there is no gable, and all the ground-floor windows are arched, along with a second coach entrance, which has also been glazed, the same as its right-hand cousin. The whole building is of painted brick; these were probably made from his own kilns close by. The inn is a Grade II listed building.

When the pub was refurbished in 2006, a number of original features were found and retained; there were some ceiling beams and fireplaces.

Sir Thomas Parkyns became known as the Wrestling Baron of Bunny, as every year on Midsummer's Day he held wrestling matches on grounds adjacent to the pub with a gold-laced hat as the prize. However, he did not take part himself – he umpired. The contest continued long after his death in 1742, until it was banned, as it was deemed to attract noisy and unruly crowds.

The hanging sign shows a stylistic R with the name beneath gold lettering on a royal blue background.

RECRUITING SERGEANT

Coltishall, Norfolk. The building is eighteenth century but with parts dating back even further, possibly the sixteenth century. Unusually there is a large clock on the outside front wall of the building.

The hanging sign shows a sergeant wearing his bright-red tunic and high shako, possibly from the late 1700's when the army needed men to fight the French.

The pub probably takes its name from the days when a recruiting sergeant toured the country attempting to enlist the locals into the army. Story has it that unscrupulous recruiters used to buy a local a pint of beer with a shilling dropped into the bottom; when the unsuspecting person had drunk his pint he was deemed to have accepted the 'King's shilling' and so joined the army or navy. The same story is told of the 'press gangs'. Glass-bottomed tankards developed from this practice.

RED HART

An unusual pub name, so called after the male of the red deer.

Bodham, Norfolk. A very old pub which started life as a beer house when Richard Jervys applied for an ale licence in 1607. The building may have just been built or converted from a pair of cottages. History is not that clear on which it was. The first possible name was the Royal Oak, which would have celebrated the restoration of the monarchy some fifty years later. Since then it has also been known as the Red Lion, although it seems that this name was used beside the Red Hart. It was also known as Commercial Hotel although that may just have been used as a general term. It was rebuilt either in the 1790s or 1800s, although exactly how much was rebuilt is not told.

The building is reputedly haunted by William Bradbury, who died in the pub of wounds sustained during an attack by a highwayman William Worsley. He usually manifests himself sitting on the end of a sleeping person's bed.

The swinging sign shows the head and shoulders of a hart dressed in a red tunic top with gold epaulets and a blue sash along with military decorations.

RED HOUSE

Knipton, Leicestershire. From the front it is a rather startling-looking three-storey red-brick Georgian building that was constructed between 1774-1790 as a private house for the Duke of Rutland's Chaplin. It then passed through various hands until it came to the estates clerk. who mortgaged it for £350. Unable to keep up payments, he sold it back to the Duke. In the 1920s the house was altered with the intention that the Duchess would live there, but this was never realised. A plan was put forward to convert the building into flats, but this also failed. Finally it was converted into a pub called the 'Red House' during the late twentieth century. The name was changed in 2005 by the 11th Duke to the Manners Arms, it being the family name.

The central front entrance is shielded by a rectangular brick porch with a mansard slate roof. It is a Grade II listed building.

The hanging sign shows the coat of arms of the Manners family, with the motto 'pour y parvenir' ('so as to accomplish').

RED LION

King William I of Scotland, who reigned from 1165 until 1214, was known as the Lion of Scotland, not because of his prowess – although that was never in question – but because he chose a red lion rampant with a forked tail for his standard. The modern Scottish banner is still a red lion rampant with a forked tail on a yellow field.

It was also the badge of John O'Gaunt, the Duke of Lancaster. The son of King Edward III and father of Henry IV, he was the most powerful figure in the realm for some thirty years and assumed this badge as a token for his claim to the throne of Castile and Leon – he was married to Constance, the daughter of Don Pedro the Cruel, of Leon and Castile.

Story has it that James I of England and VI of Scotland decreed, on his accession to the English throne in 1603, that all public buildings should display the heraldic Red Lion of Scotland in an effort to make the alliance more popular; this of course included pubs, taverns and inns.

Digswell Hill, between Datchford and Bramfield, Hertfordshire. Another favourite haunt of Dick Turpin, which until recently showed his favourite seat by the fire. Beside this old road was Sally Rainbow's Dell and the highwayman would hide within the dell, protected by her reputation as a witch.

High Wycombe, Buckinghamshire. From the portico of the pub Benjamin Disraeli made his first election address in 1832.

The inn has been demolished, but at the time of writing I believe the portico with the red lion is preserved as part of what had been Woolworth's.

Much Hadham, Hertfordshire. Monks from the nearby priory used to visit the pub using underground tunnels. One wag carved a life-sized head of a leering monk winking, which he left in a prominent place in the tunnel. Another monk, on his way back to the priory, slightly the worse for wear, saw the head and immediately dropped dead with fear. He is said to haunt the pub; his spirit has a look of sheer terror on his face.

Luton, Bedfordshire. Situated in the older part of the town centre opposite the site of the old corn exchange and market. It has a mixture of Victorian and Edwardian buildings which, I quote, 'is in a florid Edwardian style facade on a seventeenth century inn (or possibly earlier, as the Dissolution was in 1536 -41). Reputedly before the Dissolution it was the Brotherhood House of the Guild of the Holy Trinity.

In the yard travelling actors gave performances during the nineteenth century, and at one time it was also the residence of the excise officer.

Wendover, Buckinghamshire. Half-timbered with brick noggin. An original fireplace with chimney corners remains in the lounge. A stairway leads to the room where Cromwell slept in 1642 and is kept much as it was then.

Dolly Saville, ninety-nine on April 2013, and still pulling pints; she has cut back her hours, but still does three daytime shifts a week. Her determination is to celebrate a century not out. Having become something of a tourist attraction, she is always good for business. Update: Dolly made her century still pulling pints, but sadly died a few months later just short of her one hundred and first birthday.

Robert Louis Stevenson visited the house on his walk through the Chilterns in 1875 and admired the low wainscoted parlour with a fireplace and a well-worn Turkey carpet on the floor. Décor and furniture was all in keeping. He was delighted to hear a party of children singing in the street outside as they passed, which obviously pleased him to have mentioned it. Although the pub has been refurbished, one person observed that he still recognised the place from Stevenson's writings.

RED ROSE

A Red Rose was the accepted badge of the Lancastrian forces during the War of the Roses, as opposed to the White Rose of the Yorkists. A Tudor Rose was an amalgamation of both these colours, made in an effort to keep peace between the two sides.

Lindsey Tye, Suffolk. This pub is a two-storey fifteenth century Suffolk hall house and one of the county's oldest pubs, having been a local for over five hundred years.

The swinging sign shows an all-red rose, similar to a Tudor Rose but with the central petals red on a red background set in a blue circle with the name in white, all on a white background.

A hall house was usually just what it said; a large room with a central fire that had no chimney, just a hole in the roof. At one end would be the owner's quarters; at the other, the servants and kitchens. Guests would be expected to sleep round the fire in the hall.

Now renamed the Lindsey Rose.

RIBS OF BEEF

Norwich, Norfolk. Built on the banks of the River Wensum, the original building was constructed in the early 1500s, probably as a merchant's house, on the site of an earlier structure which was burned down in the great fire of Norwich in 1507. It was first called the Ribs of Beef in 1743, when it became a beer house. In 1898 part of the pub was levelled to make room for the new tram system being installed; it did not open again until six years later. In the meantime extensive modernisation had taken place. Renamed the Fye Bridge in 1919 in anticipation of the adjacent bridge being rebuilt, it retained then name until it was de-licensed in 1958, as the brewery owners considered there were too many pubs in the area. The pub then became a retail outlet for a variety of businesses, ranging from a ladies' boutique to an antique shop. In 1985 the pub was re-licensed with the original name of Ribs of Beef, which means that at least one old pub name has been rescued from obscurity.

Some years ago, during remedial work for dampness, part of the original wall was discovered; it was decided that rather than plaster over it the wall should remain on show.

RISING SUN

A sign taken from one of the badges of Edward III; his was a sunburst, i.e. rays issuing from a cloud. Later, his successor, King Richard II, used the sun in splendour, that is a full sun with a multitude of rays. Other royalty also adopted a sun at one time or another. It must be remembered that most coats of arms were altered with such occurrences as marriage, when a husband acknowledged his wife's family by incorporating a reference to them in his own badge or coat of arms.

A full sun is also incorporated into the crest of the Distillers Company. Their motto is very apt; 'drops as rain, distil as dew'!

Although royalty used the sun as an emblem, the most probable reason pubs used it was because it was an easy sign to recognise. Outside of London and other large cities, it is doubtful if the Distillers Company crest was at all known, apt though it may be for a pub.

Ickford, Buckinghamshire. A fifteenth century picture-postcard thatched two-storey building.

Inside is a single L-shaped room with partly wood floor with the remainder large tiles. Heavy beams adorn the ceiling and there is some wood covered walls; at one end is an inglenook containing an open fire that has a large steel hood.

This pub has a chair that is supposed to make any woman who sits on it pregnant. It was given national press when fourteen local women who had done just that all fell in the family way. The tally so far is supposed to be fifty-nine. One story regarding the ownership gives that it belonged to a local woman who had a large family and worked in the pub and that she haunts the chair. The hanging sign shows a smiling sun with cockerel standing on the suns head.

ROBERT BURRE

Clacton-on-Sea, Essex. In 1375 fifteen acres of land was leased from the Bishop of London-probably Simon Sudbury, who was also Lord of the Manor of Clacton – to Robert Burre, at a rent of 5/- per annum. He also had to pay 8d in lieu of services, which exempted him from the annual system of providing a certain amount of free labour to the church.

The building became a pub some time after the sixteenth century, as by that time the tenants owned around 250 acres of land.

The hanging sign shows the head and shoulders of gentleman wearing a ruff.

ROEBUCK

Roe are small, elegant deer that are native to Britain. They have a reddish-brown coat in the summer which turns grey or occasionally black in the winter. When alarmed they have a bounding gait and are very agile and quick. They are the smallest of the indigenous deer. The male is called a roebuck.

Buckhurst Hill, Essex. Until the nineteenth century this was never more than a forest alehouse with a reputation for merry making and noted for its trade dinners and bean feasts. The pleasures of the pub were extensive, which did attract a good crowd. The present building is circa 1890 with a few parts of the original retained.

The Epping Hunt, which chased mainly stag originated in King Henry II's time, when he granted the citizens of London the right to one buck in the forest at Easter.

Held on Easter Monday, it attracted large crowds and eventually degenerated into displaying a carted stag to the followers. The event was suppressed towards the end of the nineteenth century, having fallen into disrepute. Sadly this so often happened when the crowds become over-exuberant, and another custom is lost, as well as the pub, which has been demolished to make way for housing.

ROSE

In earlier times, when monks were some of the only people to offer hospitality, a rose may have been a common sign, as it symbolised the Virgin Mary. Later the colour of the rose would depend on where the pub was situated; a red rose for Lancashire and a white one for Yorkshire. The Tudor rose amalgamated both colours and so became an emblem of peace in England.

In heraldry it is quite common, both as a heraldic badge or on a coat of arms, usually red or white, while King Edward I had a gold rose with a stalk of green.

It is thought of as the queen of the flowers, although in the Middle Ages it was quite rare. A manuscript from the time of King Henry VIII carrying his signature states a red rose cost two shillings, a lot of money in King Hal's day.

In modern times a hanging sign may feature the picture of a young lady.

The saying of speaking under the rose, meaning whatever was said should remain confidential, came about when in 1586 the Pope decreed that a rose should be placed above the confessional box. As a confession was secret, the term progressively came into general use.

Bedford, Bedfordshire. It started as the Rose Inn during the sixteenth century and applied for an ale house licence in 1753, when about that time it became a coaching house with stables at the rear. According to the archives of the Duke of Bedford, it was an inn during 1546 so was actually older than thought. Since then it has had a chequered life, having been called the Rose Hotel and Commercial Inn, the Hogshead then Comptons, and finally reverting to Rose in 2018.

The present building is a three-storey nineteenth century stucco front with a Welsh slate roof and a coach entrance at one end. It is a Grade II listed building.

ROSE AND CROWN

The sign celebrates the marriage of Henry VII to Elizabeth, daughter of Edward IV, which bought to an end the War of the Roses. The crown represented the Yorkist King Henry VII, while the red rose signified the house of Lancaster.

Ashdon, Essex. Built in around 1635, it was originally farm cottages but has been a pub for at least two hundred years.

One of the ground-floor rooms still has its original wall graffiti made by some of Oliver Cromwell's prisoners of war, who were housed in that room for a time. Using soot and some dyes, the walls are covered in patterns that are still visible and on display today. On my last visit, much of the wall was covered by removable panels in order to protect the graffiti beneath.

Ellesborough, Buckinghamshire. Described as old and situated not far from Wellwick Farm, reputed home of Judge Jeffreys. Might have been his local – if the landlord would entertain him, that is. Could always have poisoned the old devil, I suppose!

Hemel Hempstead, Hertfordshire. The building was originally a butcher's shop. In 1537 the owner began brewing ale for his workers, as, with so many other times, the ale became a bigger seller than the butchers and so became an ale house.

The pub is haunted by a young girl who was crippled; she was locked in her room, so it seems, until she died. The story has been substantiated by a discovery during renovations, when a pair of shoes was found, with one sole built up so a person with one leg shorter could be more comfortable when walking. Also haunted by the ubiquitous 'Grey Lady'.

Saffron Walden, Essex. A sixteenth century inn that has a tenuous Shakespearean tradition: William G Holgate, son of the landlord in those days, was a poet and might have been the Mr WH to whom the bard dedicated the sonnets. Shakespeare did visit the town in 1607 and almost certainly stayed at the Rose and Crown.

During 1647, Oliver Cromwell and Lord Fairfax made this their headquarters and drew up the declaration of the army, which led to the trial and execution of King Charles I two years later.

Walden was famous for the saffron crocus during the Middle Ages, which gives the town its name. Tradition tells us the first crocus was bought here hidden in the staff of a Palmer from the Eastern Mediterranean, where the Greeks and Romans had known it as a dye and a valuable medicine. Palmers were those who returned home from a pilgrimage to the Holy Land with a piece of consecrated palm branch, which was usually laid at the altar of their parish church.

Tewin, Hertfordshire. Formerly used for sessions of the manorial courts.

There was a change of ownership in 1738, although no name was given. It was the meeting place of an early Hertfordshire Friendly Society.

One landlord, John Carrington, went bankrupt in 1830, since which time the premises has been owned by a brewery.

Before 1919, when the Garden City of Welwyn was created, Tewin was in open country; the village fair was held on the green outside the pub, and skittles played in what is now a store room at the back. The saloon bar, originally a tap room, has high-back settles at the hearth. where there is a discreet little hideaway known as the Poacher's Cupboard, which would suddenly be full should a gamekeeper turn up. Gamekeepers who patronised the inn knew all about this cupboard but thought better than to apprehend a poacher among his friends, particularly when having a pint.

A system upheld at the pub was the 'slate', a most civilised device to preserve confidentiality of a debt until overdue. This was not a blackboard but a proper slate hinged like a door. Debts were chalked on the inside and kept discreetly closed until Friday, pay day. If these were not cleared that evening, the hinged slate was on show for all to see. During a recent extension of the bar, the original slate was done away with in favour of a place for fuse boxes – practical, maybe, but historically dull. Now gone; as with many other things lost during refurbishment, the brewers don't know what happened to it.

The great oak door was also lost to refurbishment – that dreaded word – but the frontage is otherwise unaltered, having red and blue chequered brickwork, and the village green survives, albeit with a fringe of des res. Could have been worse – the pub could have been seen as 'ripe for development'.

Tring, Hertfordshire. The pub was built in 1906 by Lord Rothschild of Tring Park on the site of a Tudor inn. This was in response to a petition by the local people. It was leased to the Trust House Company and often used by guests of his lordship.

ROYAL HOTEL

Slough, Buckinghamshire. The Royal Hotel was built by Charles Dotesio and opened in 1842; it was used by Queen Victoria on her journey's from London to Windsor Castle until the railway branch line to Windsor opened.

The hotel was a magnificent Victorian edifice with arched windows designed in the Italian style. It was constructed from yellow brick and reputedly having some furniture from the Royal Palace at Versailles, which had been looted during the French revolution.

Sadly for the owner, when the branch line to Windsor opened, the hotel lost all the courtiers and visitors so fell into decline. Dotesio gave up the hotel and it remained empty for a number of years until it was purchased by the British Orphan Asylum in 1863.

Sadly the building was demolished in 1938.

ROYAL OAK

In early days, the oak was considered sacred, especially by the druids.

Mostly the name commemorates Charles II having hidden in an oak at Boscabel Wood with his companion Colonel Careless (or Carlis) while the Parliamentarian troops beat the wood below for him, after the Royalist defeat at Worcester in 1651. Later to commemorate his return from France, King Charles declared 29th May should be called Oak Apple Day, as it was both his birthday and the day he entered London in 1660. The tradition continued until the 1950s, even though the public holiday was abolished in 1859.

It is also the name of a ship launched at Blackwell in 1661 but which was lost on the rocks off the Scilly Isles in 1665.

There have been eight warships, all told, that have been called the Royal Oak.

Stowmarket, Suffolk. The pub is haunted by a previous landlord who appears at night on the stairs dressed in a Victorian flannel nightshirt. He seems a jovial sort of chap who has a smile and gives a wave of farewell before disappearing.

ROYAL SARACENS HEAD

Beaconsfield, Buckinghamshire. A large half-timbered corner building with a number of gables on each aspect. An eighteenth century coaching house which grew out of a tavern, it was mentioned in a will in 1510, although it is also rumoured that an inn of some sort stood on the site in 1242. Legend has it that King Richard I, after a heavy drinking session, set about the place with his battleaxe; in the morning he paid for the damage and gave permission for the Inn to be called 'Ye Royal Saracens Hedde'. Whatever the truth, it makes for a wonderful tale of how the pub got its name.

Inside is a bar and restaurant with log fires and plenty of nooks and crannies to hide away in.

An unusual feature on view is a dragon or dragging beam; this is a horizontal beam set at forty-five degrees from a corner to support the jettied floor above.

As with many other inns, it was used for other purposes, especially a coroner's court.

The hanging sign shows a cut-out of a Saracen's head with two scimitars below and the name above.

ROYAL STANDARD OF ENGLAND

Forty Green, Buckinghamshire. A further pub that lays claim to being one of the oldest inns in England, dating from the twelfth century, when it started life as an alehouse called Se Scip (The Ship).

A large, rambling building of several different building materials, mostly brick but also weatherboarding. The main parts are two-storey although other parts are of a single storey. Inside the pub is open-plan and multi-roomed, with uptight beams used as partitions, breaking it into smaller areas, several of which have church pews and long pine tables. Some of the pews have ornate carvings and there are heavy oak chairs with carved backs.

A number of rooms have open fires and there is a mixture of floor coverings, with flagstones, red quarry tiles used in addition to bricks. One entrance is made of uneven bricks and tiles, All rooms have oak beams and oak support beams, along with bare-brick walls; some ancient doors have iron grills protecting the glass which add to the effect.

The decoration is politely cluttered, with powder flasks, warming pans, bugles, swords, muskets, and pewter plates and tankards. The dark, candlelit rooms perhaps would be most atmospheric on a winter's evening in the glow of one of the open fireplaces.

The name dates from the seventeenth century when Charles II visited and, finding the innkeeper to be a Royalist, hid in the rafters when he was a fugitive after the battle of Worcester in 1651. A classic pub – and one that has been largely left alone… well, almost.

There are a number of spirits who dislike the idea of leaving the pub.

During the English Civil War twelve cavaliers were executed outside the building, including a child of twelve who is believed to have been a drummer boy. He repeatedly tugs at the sleeves of diners, described as a fair-haired thin boy who moves to some unheard sound – possibly the drum. Others include a man killed by a speeding coach outside the pub; a man who walks across the bar before disappearing through a wall and finally the shadow of a woman who haunts the ladies' toilet.

The swinging sign shows Charles II's coat of arms with the initials CR.

"A woman drove me to drink and
I never had the courtesy to thank her".

WC Fields.

ST ANNE'S CASTLE INN

Great Leighs, Essex. Claims to be the oldest inn in Essex, dating from 1171 and mentioned in the Domesday Book. However, a fire in the 1500s destroyed the thatch and much of the pub, so the present building is not that old, although still ancient.

Origin of its name is not known, nor is there a castle anywhere nearby. An old map of 1675 shows a house on the road at Leighs, beside which the name 'St Anne's' appears, this corresponds with the site of the inn. 'The Castle' part of the name maybe associated with Leez Priory, which is nearby; it is a sixteenth century mansion with a pair of crenulated turrets protecting the main entrance, very much like a castle.

On a map of 1824, the inn is marked as St Anne's Castle, and a county *Gazetteer* states the inn was formerly known as Saint Anne's where pilgrims between Walsingham and the shrine of Thomas Becket took their rest.

Beneath the pub are the remains of tunnels thought at one time to connect with the church and Leez Priory.

There are a number of ghosts haunting the place but most seem benign; one is the apparition of a small child known to have been murdered in front of her mother, possibly by her father, who then killed his wife.

One room, though, is haunted by malicious spirits; as the occupant sleeps the room becomes icy cold, the bedclothes are pulled from the bed and on occasions the curtains are ripped. Dark shapes with wicked-looking faces surround the bed. After 1563, when the Witchcraft Act was passed by Parliament, Essex hanged and burnt at the stake a large number of 'witches', some around this village. One was executed then buried under a boulder at Scrap Faggot Green where several lanes join; Scrap Faggot being the old Essex name for a witch.

During WWII, when large military trucks could not easily get round the Green because of the boulder, it was bulldozed to ease their passage, after which odd things began to happen. Livestock belonging to farmers was switched in the night, which could not have been done by practical jokers – the noise would have given them away. At the inn, handles were rattled on locked doors when nobody was there and a drayman, scared by 'something' in the cellar, refused to deliver.

At one time the inn sign showed a skull wearing a mitre representing Thomas, together with the date of his birth and a scene of pilgrims coming over a hill.

SARACEN'S HEAD

An Arab or Moslem, the infidel Turk, a symbol which many knights adopted on their armorial bearings on return from the Crusades.

Etymology: from the Late Latin 'sacracenus'. meaning those people who harassed the eastern borders of the Roman Empire. Later became to mean infidel, unbeliever or pagan especially during the Crusades.

Part of the coat of arms of the Shirley family, the Earl Ferrers.

Sir Anthony Shirley (or Sherley), 1565-1635, went on a trade mission to Persia and returned as the Shah's envoy in an unsuccessful attempt to form an alliance against the Turks. This might account for the Saracen in his coat of arms.

The Shirley family motto is 'Loyal je suis' ('I have loyalty').

Ettington Park near Stratford on Avon belongs to the family, as does/did Staunton Harold Hall in Leicestershire. This manor, given to the Ferrers by William the Conqueror, is still owned by the Shirleys today, who have had it in their keeping for five hundred years. They added the Barony of Ferrers to their title in Charles II's day and have since raised it to an earldom. It is now a Cheshire home.

Lawrence, Earl Ferrers, was the last aristocrat to be hanged in England, during 1760 on a modern type of gallows that was being used for the first time. There was no silken cord of legend: it was hemp. Having murdered his steward

John Johnson and fled, he was apprehended and taken to a pub at Ashby-de-la-Zouche. Later put on trial before his peers at Westminster, he was hanged at Tyburn, his petition as a peer to be beheaded having been refused.

Great Dunmow, Essex. Eighteenth century facade with the old inn behind, probably dating from 1600. Landlords are recorded from 1620: one of the earliest was a Roundhead who fought with Cromwell. Another, an apparently worthy and pious man, was a highwayman who robbed his guests as soon as they left. He was also hand in glove with smugglers – Dunmow was a smuggling centre in those days, being near handy Essex creeks. Many cargoes are sure to have found their way to his inn.

A later landlord, Edward Bettes harboured Roger Banstead and Thomas Lawrence in spite of the local constable's warning. They robbed Bettes of £8 in money and goods. The pair were known to the law but there was little evidence against them. It was not recorded if they were captured this time, though possibly they were since details of the crime have been noted.

Southwell, Nottinghamshire. Also known as Southwell Minster, being the one village in England with a cathedral.

The Saracen's Head is Tudor, timber-framed and the village's oldest inn, with deeds dating from 1341. The doors to the courtyard are five hundred years old.

The former Assembly Rooms next door is now the hotel dining room, but the inn's interior has suffered generally from modern hands.

On his way to raise his standard at Nottingham, Charles I slept in the oaken four-poster, and again on the way back before surrendering to the Scots at Newark in May 1646. His last night of freedom was spent here and his final meal taken in the coffee room before his arrest.

At the time of the King's visits, the inn was the King's Head, but the name was changed to the Saracen's Head after the King's execution to show allegiance to Cromwell. (Choice of name doesn't say much for Cromwell!) Another source tells that the name was changed because Charles I was executed with a Saracen's sword. Yet another story relates that the name was changed because of Charles II swarthy features.

Thomas Moore, the Irish poet, was a guest here in 1828, being often visited by the teenage Byron. It is known that after overcoming his shyness, Byron would come and go frequently, making himself at home. His signature on a wall has been preserved.

The hotel is reputed to be haunted by both King Charles I and the poet Lord Byron.

Ware, Hertfordshire. The Great Bed of Ware, ten feet wide and eleven feet long, was at one time in the inn, afterwards being used during local festivals and owned by a succession of Ware innkeepers – at the George, the Crown and finally the Saracen's Head, where it remained until 1870.

According to popular tradition, it was made by Jonas Fosbrooke, a journeyman carpenter of Ware who presented it to King Edward IV in 1463. When his son was murdered in 1483 it was sold. The date 1483 is painted on the headboard and might seem to verify the tale, but the bed is actually thought to have been made as a publicity stunt for the White Hart at Ware around 1590. It was famous enough by the time it was mentioned by Shakespeare in 'Twelfth Night', first performed in 1601. It was then sold to the proprietor of the Rye House Hotel at Hoddesdon and acquired by the V&A in 1931.

SCOLE INN

Scole, near Diss, Norfolk. Dating from 1655, built as a coaching inn and formerly called the White Hart. It is a Grade I listed building.

The foyer is at the back, where it could be conjectured the coaches stopped; it has four ancient wooden pillars with an original balcony rail on either side of the entrance which leads to the main staircase, this was hand carved in the 1600s. With plenty of old beams and fireplaces, the whole place exudes history.

When still the White Hart, the inn had the largest sign ever known, though today there seems to be little mention made of this. It was the most extensive and expensive so far seen. Commissioned in 1655 by James Peck of Norwich, it was dedicated to 'James Bett, Gentleman, by his most obedient servant Harwin Martin'. The sign was made by J Fairchild at a cost of £1,057. It depicted twenty-five different scenes, and it spanned the road, resting on a pier of bricks at one side and against the house on the other. It also showed the arms of the chief towns and gentlemen of the county along with biblical scenes and characters from mythology. All was carved from wood and it remained in place for almost a hundred and fifty years until taken down circa 1795. Alas, nothing remains today. Gone too is the massive round bed in the White Hart which could accommodate forty people – so long as they slept with their feet towards the centre. How else?

Famous people reputed to have stayed include Charles II and Nell Gwyn, and Nelson with Lady Hamilton.

The pub is haunted by a woman called Emma, who was murdered here by her husband because he thought she had been unfaithful to him. She appears wearing a grey dress and bonnet and is always crying.

Another spirit reputed to haunt the place is the highwayman John Belcher who, when pursued by the authorities, is said to have rode up the great staircase before escaping from the top floor. He manifests himself occasionally, and the rattle of horses' hoofs are heard at the rear of the pub.

SEVEN WIVES

St Ives, Cambridgeshire. Built in 1962. The hanging sign and the bargeboard above the front door are stylised white outlines of seven women in a row above the pub name, all on a blue/green background.

The pub takes its name from the riddle;

> As I was going to St. Ives, I met a man with seven wives,
> Every wife had seven sacks,
> Every sack had seven cats,
> Every cat had seven kitts.
> Kitts, cats, sacks, wives,
> How many were going to St Ives?

The question is, of course, a trick; the answer being at least one. As the narrator was going to St Ives, the other company was coming from the town.

SHIP

One of the earliest signs and one with a number of explanations. It was early associated with the Ark, for which reason the sign was carried round the country for purposes of adoration. This is one reason given for the Ship sign being found inland as well as by rivers and ports.

In many country places, though, the word 'sheep' was pronounced 'ship' and the inns which bear this name are often very far from the sea or ports, and in obvious sheep-rearing country. Another derivation is said to be from the northern dialect word 'shippen', meaning a cowshed.

Only when the inn is at or very near a port can it be assumed the ship is the seafaring sort. Often when this is the case, the picture of a vessel with its name will be painted on the sign.

Grendon Underwood, Buckinghamshire. This inn of sixteenth century origin, later privately owned and known as Shakespeare Farm, is said to have been where Shakespeare stayed on his journeys to and from London. According to John Aubrey, the antiquary, it is here he might have written 'A Midsummer Night's Dream' and 'Much Ado About Nothing'. Later accounts state Shakespeare's inspiration for Dogberry and Verges came from two characters he met at the inn. The sign of the Ship now hangs in Aylesbury Museum. The farmhouse with timbered and brick framework is gabled and has windows containing the original lattice and leaded glass.

SIGNAL BOX

Cleethorpes, Lincolnshire. This inn, originally a signal box, is situated at the town end of the Cleethorpes Coast Light Railway, a two-kilometre-long fifteen-inch gauge railway which runs along the sea front to Humberston North Sea Lane.

A recent opening and a contender for the smallest pub in England, with an area of eight by eight; it can accommodate only six people but is more of a tap room than an inn: the main drinking area is outside.

SILVER LION

Lilley, Hitchin, Hertfordshire. A heraldic reference to the local Sowerby family, who were wealthy merchants from Hatton Gardens. They bought the pub and Putteridge Park in the middle of the nineteenth century, along with Lilley village and other pubs nearby. One of the family, Colonel Sowerby. was killed by an Egyptian stag in Putteridge Park during 1888.

An early tenant was James Pates, who also worked as a wheelwright; he was tenant from 1855 until his death thirty years later.

Lilley has a confusing address; it comes under the Luton Unitary Authority, which is in Bedfordshire; however, the village is actually in Hertfordshire. To cloud the waters even more, Putteridge Park, although in Hertfordshire, is the campus for the University of Bedfordshire. The mind boggles!

SIX BELLS

St Albans, Hertfordshire. A sixteenth century inn within the walls of the old town. During excavations, an eighteenth century kiln that made bricks used to construct the houses was found near the inn. Also identified were remnants of a butchery and kitchen from the twelfth century which indicated existence of a hostel servicing pilgrims visiting the cathedral. Further exploration uncovered Roman pottery and large amounts of rare painted wall plaster, along with the remains of a Roman hotel dating back 1,500 years, probably the earliest and largest building of that period discovered.

SIXTEEN STRING JACK

Theydon Bois, Essex. The inn is named after a local highwayman, John Rann, a notorious dandy who earned his nickname from the sixteen silken strings which dangled at the knees of his breeches. He liked to frequent Bagnigge Wells the London pleasure gardens. On one occasion, after paying unwanted attention to a lady in the ballroom, he was pitched out of a window into the Fleet below. His taste for high living caused his downfall, for he turned to highway robbery to pay for extravagant tastes. He was arrested and tried on six different occasions, but each time was acquitted. Finally the law caught up with him and he was hanged at Newgate Prison on 30th November, 1774. He dined in style with friends before he went to the gallows in a pea-green costume.

The sign depicted a stylishly dressed rogue being hauled off to the gallows.

The pub is no more, being demolished to make way for housing. It was the only one of this name, so another story from history will probably be lost.

SOLE BAY INN

Southwold, Suffolk. Close to the lighthouse and the nearest pub to the town's brewery.

An indecisive sea battle was fought off the town in 1672 during the Dutch Wars. English and French ships commanded by James, Duke of York, were attacked by the Dutch fleet commanded by de Ruyter, who eventually retired.

Although not a traditional bay, the sea area opposite Southwold is called Sole Bay, or it was in the 1950s and '60s.

SOUTH END

Kempston, Bedfordshire. The sign shows a couple of children playing on a beach, which is apt as the nearest seaside resort is probably Southend-on-Sea in Essex. It could, of course, be that the area of Kempston where the pub is situated is known as the south end!

SPADE OAK

Well End, near Marlow, Buckinghamshire. Originally built in 1887 and then called Ye Ferry Hotel as there was a regular ferry service across the river from here.

In the vicinity is Spade Oak Farm, from which perhaps the inn took its name, if the farm came first, that is. A spade farm was one that was cultivated by hand; also a spade tree was a dialect word for the shaft of a spade, either which could have been corrupted.

A three-storey black-and-white Victorian building with high ceilings. An attractive patio is alongside set with tables and benches.

SPORTSMAN'S ARMS

Witham, Essex. This timber-framed pub claims to date from about 1300 but the main fabric is sixteenth century, although there is a plaque on the front of the building stating AD 1300. It was in 1653 that Samuel Wall from Witham issued a token which displayed a double-headed eagle, from which it can be deduced he was the landlord of the inn.

There is a mysterious well on the premises, the entry to which can only be made from the roof. It would be more than likely to have been used by smugglers who lowered various kegs down this, the whereabouts of which would be unbeknown to many. Since the landlord must have known about it, you can be assumed he was turning a blind eye to unusual visitors – or was it a deaf ear to any unaccountable strange noises?

On my last visit the pub was closed and looked very sorry for itself.

STAR

An ensign of knightly rank. A star of some form constitutes part of almost every order of knighthood.

It is also a religious symbol referring to the Bethlehem star, or to the Virgin Mary. Traditionally in many country areas, if the church was dedicated to Saint Mary the nearest inn or public house was often called the Star.

Bishop's Stortford, Hertfordshire. A seventeenth century timber-framed building with a Victorian façade. Reputedly haunted by the ubiquitous 'Grey Lady'.

Standon, Hertfordshire. A seventeenth century pub with two bars, the public bar being sports-orientated whilst the other is more of a lounge-cum-dining area.

Some years ago when the landlord opened the door to the bar he saw a group of a dozen or so men, all wearing tricorne hats and accompanied by a lady of Latin appearance. They were all being very jolly, laughing and drinking. When the landlord was noticed they all disappeared.

The man, being inquisitive, closed the door and looked through a window into the bar; to his amazement the people had returned, along with a further lady.

At the rear is a garden, and the swinging sign shows a three-dimensional painted star.

STONE JUG

Clophill, Bedfordshire. This was the type of jug in which the labourers in fields were supplied beer to keep them going on the long summer days.

STRAWPLAITERS

Luton, Bedfordshire. During the reign of James I, Luton was the centre of the straw-plaiting industry, when woven straw ribbons were supplied to hat manufacturers. Gradually hats made of felt replaced those entirely made of straw. When the fashion for wearing hats decreased, so the trade in the town also died.

STUMP AND CANDLE

Boston, Lincolnshire. Formerly the Rum Puncheon. Takes its name from the famous church in the town, nicknamed 'The Boston Stump', which is a 272-

foot tower that ends in an octagonal lantern instead of the usual spire. A candle is of course associated with the church.

This inn bears a Blue Plaque in memory of John Foxe, the martyrologist, who was born here in 1516. His history of the church has become known as *The Book of Martyrs*.

SUGAR LOAF

The normal method of marketing refined sugar until the early 1800s was as a conical solid block. It originally advertised a grocer but was also visually attractive to tavern keepers, who have been using it as a sign since the seventeenth century.

One further possibility is the pub may be called after a hill of that name which is shaped similar to a sugar loaf.

Luton, Bedfordshire. A two-storey corner pub in the old part of Luton, probably built in the mid-nineteenth century when the town expanded. Inside is a single L-shaped room with the foot of the L up several steps to the bar and small area where the locals congregate. The other part of the room has back-to-back banquettes, making small booths. Dark wood below the dado and at the front of the bar, along with Art Deco leaded glass lampshades, which help to give a warm feeling to the room. A real locals' pub.

The swinging sign shows a sugar loaf.

Market Harborough, Leicestershire. Dating from the early 1700s, when it was a grocer's shop. In 1910 it was owned by Thomas Goward who. along with his family and servants, lived on the premises. A fire that year almost destroyed the building; all bar one of the occupants escaped unhurt. One of the shop workers died in the fire; he subsequently haunts the pub. When he manifests he is wearing scorched clothing and has burns on his face.

SUN

Along with the moon, the sun was of pagan origin, representing Apollo and Diana in mythology. As it was a sign easy to paint and one everyone would recognise, it and its derivatives naturally became popular. Its popularity was helped along by several kings adopting as their emblem; Richard II and III, and Edward VI.

It is also a device in the arms of the Distillers Company, which were granted in 1638. Sometimes under the picture was the line; 'The best ale under the sun'.

Dedham, Essex, Right on the border with Suffolk, a two-storey one-time coaching inn in the middle of John Constable country. A building on this site was recorded in the Domesday Book, although the present building is fifteenth-century.

Haunted by a girl called Elsa, who worked at the inn but was hanged in the pub yard on the orders of the Witchfinder General Matthew Hopkins, who wreaked havoc in the county during his dreadful reign. She has been seen inside, and outside the pub with a bundle of clothes, always dressed in a black cloak, or even holding a door open for a customer.

The hanging sign shows a smiling sun in all its glory.

Between 1644 and 1646 Essex had a terrible reputation for executing witches; three hundred were executed after being interrogated and tortured by the Witchfinder General and his accomplice John Stern (spellings vary).

He died in August 1847 in Manningtree, Essex, possibly of tuberculosis, although historian James Sharpe said a 'pleasing legend' about Hopkins' death told that he died after being subjected to his own swimming test he used on witches!

If the story is true, it was poetic justice!

Hitchin, Hertfordshire. A well-preserved building of blue brick with rubble-brick dressings and a central carriageway which leads the courtyard and an assembly room which was added in 1770. It is a traditional inn with an arch, courtyard and stables in the form of a large U. The entrance to the hotel is on one leg of the U, this having a portico supported by two columns which is where the coach passengers would enter. There is no front entrance.

A sixteenth century coaching inn which was once HQ of Parliamentary Troops housed in town during English Civil War. Haunted by cries of 'mind your head' when there is no one about; also a monk who walks across the room then goes behind the bar and helps himself to a drink.

In 1772, three robbers tied up the landlord and robbed the place. Stupidly, they scratched their initials and the date of the robbery in the brickwork next to the front door; that evidence allowed the constable to catch them. They still haunt the inn.

Saffron Walden, Essex. The gables are decorated with seventeenth century pargetting, which is the East Anglian art of moulding relief motifs in plaster on walls. It tells the story of Tom Hickathrift, armed with a wheel for a shield, battering the Giant of the Smeeth. Tom, an eleven foot Cambridgeshire giant, conformed to all the clichés; large appetite, unlimited prowess and educationally subnormal. His job was to deliver beer from King's Lynn. He objected the long detour to avoid the Wisbech giant, so one day he strode straight across the no-go area. Out comes the giant, displaying severed heads and wielding a club. Tom ripped the wheel off his brewer's cart to use as a shield and one of the axles as a club. After a lengthy set-to, Tom's youth and stamina won. Tom found the monster's cave full of treasure, enough to last a lifetime. This made him a hero and he became known as Mr Thomas Hickathrift throughout East Anglia.

SWAN (INN)

Favourite badge of a number of monarchs, as well as other families. Godfrey of Bouillon, circa 1060-1100, was the grandson of the Swan Knight, who came to save his grandmother, the Duchess of Bouillon, from the clutches of Renier, Duke of Saxony. He arrived in an enchanted boat drawn by a chained swan. The story has been localised to augment the status of various families, although similar stories abound throughout Europe, especially in Germany where Godfrey is replaced by Lohengrin.

Edward III used this bird on his tunic and shield for a tournament held at Canterbury in 1349. Henry IV; Thomas Woodstock, the Duke of Gloucester; and Cecily Neville, the Duchess of York, mother of Edward IV and Richard III, also had a swan as a supporter.

Depicted in the arms of Henry V together with an antelope. Also an emblem of the Vintners Company and used by the early printer Wynkyn de Worde.

In ancient times the swan was a symbol of innocence because of its colour.

Amersham, Buckinghamshire. A coaching inn which claims to have been rebuilt in 1643 on the site of an earlier inn. The date 1671 is on a chimney.

Brentwood, Essex. The most haunted part of the inn is an upstairs room, where it is believed William Hunter, a Protestant, spent his last night. He was a young man of nineteen who was imprisoned in the Swan before his execution. According to an account left by his brother, William had a dream the night before he was taken to the stake in which he foresaw events of the following day; how he met his father, who pleaded with him, and how when he was taken to the market place, the sheriff showed him a letter from the Queen saying he would be spared if he recanted his faith. Both happened as foreseen, but William refused and suffered. Since then his spirit has often revisited the place of his imprisonment.

Other odd things happen. Copper plates roll along a shelf as if being pushed, and bumping sounds come from the cellars. Furniture is moved about at night, and lights switched on and off. Many people have mentioned there is something odd about the stairs leading from the cellar to the top of the building, such as drops in temperature and the feeling of not being alone.

Bromham, Bedfordshire. First licensed as a pub during 1798 and became a coaching inn which was positioned near a toll gate so coaches stopped there anyway. It is stone-built, comfortable inside with log fires and a garden with a patio area outside.

So called due to the proximity of the River Ouse and the multitude of swans on the river.

Horning, Norfolk. A legend runs that on the 21st July every five years, the spirit of the Lord Abbot of St Benet's re-enacts the ceremony of the crowning of Ella, said to have been an early King of the Angles. He was known as the Swan of Peace. A hundred yards downstream from the pub you may witness the event.

Hoxne, Suffolk, pronounced Hoxen. This has been a public house since 1619. The original building was erected for the benefit of the Bishop of Hoxne in the early sixteenth century on the site of Oakley Park, earlier known as Hoxne Hall, which stood on the site of the original bishop's palace, of which there is no trace.

The front and gable ends were rebuilt in brick in the eighteenth century, but exposed Tudor timbers are visible at the back. The original carriage entry which had a room over it was where the car park is now. When originally built it was possible to walk from one end to the other on the ground floor, but the first floor was divided into three sections, each with its own staircase which suggest it was a guests' lodging house. Legend says, all lodgers were ladies, who were guests of the bishop.

The main bar has a heavy oak floor with tables down the sides and an imposing fireplace at one end surrounded by armchairs. The dining room has a beamed ceiling, leading off which is a number of rooms and passages. The whole place retains its original period atmosphere.

Lavenham, Suffolk. Correct age unknown of this timbered house with diamond-leaded panes, it is at least five hundred years old.

There are fine examples of timber framing from the reign of both Queen Elizabeth's, as old building technique was copied for a 1965 extension in order to retain architectural symmetry.

One of the town's three guild halls, the Wool Hall which has survived from the fourteenth century, is now an extension at the back of the inn. The inn has uneven floors, great upright timbers and many exposed beams with large open fireplaces. On the ceiling beams are signatures, decorations and brevets of soldiers and airmen who gathered here from airfields and army camps nearby during WWII.

Radwell, Bedfordshire. This thatched, seventeenth century building has brick buttresses supporting the stone walls. A two-bar pub with stone floors and oak beams inside with a well-lived-in atmosphere. A lovely example of a country pub.

Another pub which takes its name from the birds on the nearby River Ouse.

Sible Hedingham, Essex. In 1863, an eighty-year-old deaf mute nicknamed 'Old Dummy' was accused of casting a spell. Villagers dragged the old man from the bar of the Swan and threw him into the nearby stream in accordance with the ancient belief that water, the element that baptised him, would reject a witch. Guilt was considered proven if the subject floated and innocence established if they sank. Old Dummy struggled in the water under a hail of stones until someone hauled him out. He died several days later in the local workhouse.

> I feel no pain, dear mother, now
> But oh! I am so very dry.
> O take me to a brewery
> And leave me there to die.
>
> *Anon.*

THREE CRANES

A sign showing birds was possibly a pun on the cranes used by vintners to lift barrels of wine into the cellars. On the other hand, the name might be a corruption of the Three Crawns, or skulls, relating to the Magi, which were at one time kept in Cologne Cathedral.

Turvey, Bedfordshire. A seventeenth century coaching inn. Part of the building is brick and stone, and the rest has mock-Tudor beams and is painted white. A beer garden at the rear leads to a brook.

The hanging sign shows three cranes heads in a shield.

THREE CROWNS

There are a number of interpretations for this name; as a reference to James I, as he was the first monarch to rule over three kingdoms – England, Scotland and Wales. Another likely one is as a biblical allusion to the Three Kings who visited Jesus at Bethlehem.

Others are also a possible corruption of Three Crawns, or skulls, the relics of the Magi believed to have been brought from Milan to Cologne Cathedral in the twelfth century. One medieval legend calls them the Three Kings of Cologne.

In heraldry, the sign refers to the Worshipful Company of Drapers, whose arms were granted in 1364. Three crowns was the guild emblem of drapers, so a pub named such could indicate the landlord's second trade.

A five-shilling piece was known as a crown and some signs depict three of these.

Redhill, Nottinghamshire. Elizabeth Sheppard, a seventeen-year-old, was murdered on her way to seek work in Mansfield. Her murderer was a scissors grinder named Charles Rotherham who thought she had money. He left her shoes behind in the room he had stayed in but was caught ten days after he had tried to sell her umbrella at the inn. He was later hanged at Gallows Hill. Her ghost is said to haunt the spot at Harlow Wood where she died in July 1817. Her memorial, which has become known as the Bessie Stone, is near the junction of the A60 and B6020, and she is believed to appear whenever it is moved.

THREE DROVERS

Crowland, Lincolnshire. This pub takes its name from a grisly story told many years ago.

A traveller knocked at an inn seeking shelter; the landlord had one room available which she said 'was not used' but he could occupy if he wished. During the night he was disturbed by a knock on the door, which he at first ignored, but when it was repeated, he opened it only to find the passage empty. When this happened again a little later, he called out, asking who it was. At this, three apparitions glided into the room. They told him they were drovers who had been murdered by the landlord for their money; he had then buried them in the back yard. The man followed them outside, where a spot was pointed out. Next day, he sought the help of a local man and paid him to dig at the spot. Three bodies were found. The constable was called and the landlord arrested. He was so shocked by the way in which his crime had been discovered that he confessed and was later hanged.

Amongst papers of the Huddleston family of Cambridge was an encounter with three ghosts written by a certain Isaac Kirton, who was later identified as a member of the family. It dates from the early part of eighteenth century. The same story?

THREE GOATS

Lincoln, Lincolnshire. From the Old English *'geotan'* ('to pour'). This name is possibly a corruption of the Three Gowts, a dialect word for a drain or sluice, as these at one time conducted water into a large lake, the Swan Pool, now called Brayford Pool, then on to the River Witham. The name of the inn has been changed to the Black Goats.

THREE HAMMERS

St Albans, Hertfordshire. Three hammers feature on the arms of the Worshipful Company of Blacksmiths granted to them in 1571.

In 1838, the original premises was a tavern with a blacksmith's shop attached.

THREE HORSESHOES

Warham, Norfolk. Originally a smithy with stables at the back where the blacksmith would have sold ale to customers while horses were reshod.

The inn was part of the Holkham estate, property owned by the Earls of Leicester. It was sold in the 1960s together with four adjoining cottages, these are now lost to a car park.

It is virtually unchanged since the 1930s. Beer is still served from the cask, two rooms leading off the bar retain their original features and one landlord who took over replaced the fluorescents with gas mantles.

In the bar, a simple game, the Norfolk Twister, is played. This is a wheel mounted on the ceiling divided into segments. A central pointer is spun with the hand, the game being to bet on which number or colour the pointer will stop. Fortunately the ceilings are low.

THREE TUNS

From the Old English 'tunne' ('a barrel or large cask or trunk'). The original meaning did not specify any particular size, nor for any particular product.

The Arms of the Worshipful Company of Vintners contain three tuns with a chevron, along with a motto, *'Vinum exhilarat animum'* ('Wine gladdens the spirit'). They were granted their charter in 1363 along with the monopoly of trade with Gascony, not only in wine, but other goods as well. The Company is ranked eleventh in precedence in the Guilds of the City of London. They were at one time allowed to sell wine without a licence within three miles of the city walls and in certain ports and towns on the road from Dover to London.

The contents of a tun has varied over time; in the fifteenth century it was 252 gallons, then became a loose term of 256, 240 or 208 gallons. However, the mighty tun in Heidelberg Castle holds 58,000 gallons, so it was never an exact size.

Bungay, Suffolk. Late-seventeen century posting house and commercial hotel built on the site of an earlier building dating from the mid-sixteenth century which was destroyed by fire 140 years later.

Claims to be haunted by at least twenty-four ghosts. One, Rex Bocon, who worked in the pub and whose father was the local vicar, in 1682 murdered his wife and her lover before hanging himself. When he appears he has a sorrowful expression.

Another is a highwayman called Tom Hardy who used to frequent the pub; he was caught and hanged, but his spirit returned to the pub. When he appears he is wearing a long dark cloak, tricorne hat and has a brace of pistols in his belt.

The hanging sign shows three gold tuns with the name above also in gold.

TICKELL ARMS

Thomas Tickell, 1686-1740, was a poet and translator. He was Fellow of Queen's College, Oxford, and was Under Secretary to Joseph Addison in 1717 and later Secretary to the Lords Justices of Ireland.

Whittlesford, Cambridgeshire. This village pub was once a country house that was built about 1700. Its unusual blue-washed exterior is overrun with honeysuckle and roses with a conservatory opening onto a terrace. It has altogether a faded elegance echoed in the two high-ceilinged bars in traditional brown with a large garden that has an overgrown trout pond with a fountain.

The innkeeper at one time was the eccentric Kim or Joseph Hollick de la Taste Tickell, who had been many things, including an amateur actor, before becoming the bizarre landlord. Each morning he would bathe naked in the pond then walk through the bar dripping algae. When dressed he would sport knee breeches and buckled shoes; he built up a clientele of students and dons from Cambridge universities. His policy of turning away those he considered improperly dressed helped to preserve his pub with air of genteel days gone by.

The pub was also famous for the food he served, equally as eccentric as the landlord, but was ahead of its time. All the same, the public loved it.

A handwritten notice outside the pub listed those banned; left-wingers, long hairs, CND-ers, jean-wearers etc. In 1970 he appeared in court after having armed himself with a medieval weapon taken from the wall of his pub, emerging outside ready to take on anyone who disapproved of the way he ran his business. Perhaps objections had arisen from his dislike also of 'modern' women and female workers from a local factory, whom he claimed lowered the tone of the village. Refusing to serve them due to their bad language, they argued it was no worse than that heard outside his pub on closing time – and at times from Mine Host himself. On one occasion they debagged him – which he didn't seem to mind.

If ever a borderline customer asked for the loo, Tickell was in the habit of saying, "Along the corridor, turn left, you'll see a sign saying Gentlemen, but in your case we will make an exception."

Kim Tickell died in 1990.

TIN HAT

Hinckley, Leicestershire. A modern estate pub opened in the 1980s, it got its name from a competition for that purpose. The town has been known as 'Tin 'At' since sometime in the nineteenth century, when a sheep drover boasted he could drink a hatful of ale. To put the boast to the test, the landlord had a local blacksmith make one up; this hat held over four gallons. The story does not relate if the drover completed the task or who paid for the ale!

A further explanation has been put forward that it originated from a bucket which was placed over one of the town's water pumps in order to keep it clean.

A tin hat appears on the town coat of arms.

TIN POT INN

Wheathampstead, Hertfordshire. Built originally as a medieval Hall House in the late fifteenth or early sixteenth century, it is now a Grade II listed building.

In 1900 the annual rent was £15, rising to £25 by 1917. My! How things have changed in the past hundred years!

Reputed to be haunted by Lady Katherine Ferres, who turned to being a highwayman (woman) after her husband squandered her fortune. She preyed on travellers crossing the nearby Nomansland Common; she was shot one night while attempting a robbery there.

The name of the pub is rather interesting, as 'tin pot' means something that is second rate, or worthless. So to call your pub by that name seems rather deprecating to say the least.

TRIPLE PLEA

Halesworth, Suffolk. Much is of interest in the sign. An old man is surrounded by his parson, a doctor and a lawyer, with the devil peeking from behind a curtain in the background. Each man is pleading his is the greater cause: the parson for his soul, the doctor for his life and the lawyer for the estate. The devil's expression suggests he knows the answer.

The triple plea as in verse goes;

> Law, Physic and Divinity,
> Being in dispute could not agree
> To settle which among them three
> Should have the superiority.

> Law pleads he does preserve men's lands
> And all their goods from ravener's hands,
> Therefore of right he challenged – he

> Physic proscines receipts for health
> (Which men prefer before their wealth)

> Then straight steps up the Priest demur,
> Who of mens souls hath care and cure;
> Therefore of right he challenged – he
> Should have the superiority.

> If Judges end this 'Triple Plea',

The Lawyer shall bear all the sway.

It Umpires then their verdicts give,
Physicians are best of all who live.

If Bishops arbitrate the case,
The Priest must have the higher place.

But if honest sober wise men judge,
Then all the three away may trudge.
But if men fools and knaves may be.
They'll be ass-ridden by all three.

Now if them three cannot agree,
The Devil shall ride them three by three.

TWENTY CHURCHWARDENS

Cockley Cley, Norfolk. The village school here was closed in the 1930s; after serving as a chapel and storeroom, it was linked to two adjoining cottages and converted to an inn, replacing one which had been closed. Bishop Hugh Blackburne, then the rector, suggested the name; he was just joining his group of parishes, making the total up to ten and bringing the number of his churchwardens to twenty.

Invited to attend the opening, each was presented with a tankard engraved with the name of his parish, together with a long-stemmed clay pipe, known in the nineteenth century as a 'churchwarden'.

These items, kept on display at the pub, are made use of as required, the tankard being the most popular.

When the church tower collapsed the bar was used for services for three years.

TWIN FOXES

Stevenage New Town, Hertfordshire. England's first new town under the New Town Act of 1946 and built to cater for London's overspill. The old town, which is on the Great North Road, dated from Norman times.

The inn was opened in 1953 in the Bedwell area of Stevenage; it was named after two famous poachers who were born in 1857. They poached all over Hertfordshire, beginning their poaching career in 1871 with a stolen gun.

Born at Symonds Green, they were named after the Ebenezer Chapel on Albert Street, of which their father was a devout supporter and lay preacher. They were identical physically although of different character. Ebenezer Albert was taciturn and spent much time in the local taverns. Albert Ebenezer was good-natured with a vein of humour, which entertained magistrates and public alike during his frequent appearances in court. Being identical, the brothers always had an alibi, covering for each other on many occasions. Both men were popular.

Edward VII, then Prince of Wales, is known to have waited at the inn after his car had broken down. He was greatly entertained by the tales they told.

Ebenezer, sixty-nine, died in 1926 due to leaving his hospital bed to have a last look at the coverts where he had spent his life. Albert died at eighty in 1937 in hospital, and up to the last he was visited by the local gentry whom he called his friends, despite some of them having contributed to his 120 convictions for poaching.

Sir Edward Henry used twins, including the Foxes, to prove an individual could be identified by his fingerprints. Later made Chief Commissioner for the London Metropolitan Police, his work, together with Francis Galton, was introduced into Scotland Yard in 1901 as the Galton-Henry system.

The sign shows the brothers in silhouette, with guns and a dog on one side and a pair of fox heads on the other.

TUDOR OAKS

Astwick, Bedfordshire. This pub was at one time a farmhouse and then an ice-cream factory. In the sixteenth or seventeenth century it stood on the turnpike now the Great North Road, where it is said the Yeomen of the Guard on their way to York stopped for sustenance. The interior has a fine Jacobean staircase, beams in the bars and several open fireplaces. As it originated as a farmhouse, the name today might reflect the many oak beams used when first built.

TUMBLEDOWN DICK

This usually refers to Richard Cromwell, 1626-1712, the least popular of Oliver's sons, and has come to describe vacillation of the worst sort or anything which will not stand. He served in Fairfax's New Model Army with little distinction and was the opposite of everything his father wished him to be: idle, a spendthrift, in debt and, worst of all, one who gave religion the blind eye. Although Oliver began to include him in affairs of state, Richard was inept, and on succeeding his father, for which he was not ready, he was forced from office after crass errors of judgement in 1659. On the Restoration of the monarchy, he was forced into exile.

As there is an English dance tune with this name, it may be to that that the name refers.

Woodton, Norfolk. The sign shows Diogenes on one side and a drunken man on the other, with the ditty;

> Now Diogenes Is dead and laid in his tomb,
> Tumbledown Dick is come to his room.

TURPIN'S CAVE

Epping Forest, Hertfordshire. This public house was just below High Beech in Epping Forest. It was on the site of a large cave where a housing estate is now prominent. Whether or not Dick Turpin used the one-time cave is unconfirmed.

> Guesting awhile in the rooms of a beautiful inn;
> Glad till the dancing stops and the lilt of the music ends;
> Laugh till the game be played – and be you merry, my friends.

> *John Masefield.*

UNICORN

The Royal Arms of Scotland had two as supporters. Brought into the Royal Arms of Great Britain by James I when one replaced the Welsh dragon put there by Henry VII.

In earlier times, it was often the sign of an apothecary, as the horn of the unicorn was believed to be the antidote for all poisons. It features in the arms of Worshipful Company of Apothecaries, granted in 1617.

The name was given by fishermen to the narwhal, which has a single, long fluted tusk. There are many allusions to this animal in the Old Testament; It was believed that a unicorn could only be caught by a virgin, and was sometimes depicted with its head resting on the lap of the Virgin Mary, which was symbolic of Jesus being born of a virgin.

Features in the arms of the Worshipful Company of Wax Chandlers, granted 1483 and the Worshipful Company of Goldsmiths, granted 1327.

A Scottish gold coin of the fifteenth/sixteenth centuries was known as a unicorn.

Langar, Nottinghamshire. Scrope Viscount Howe was Member of Parliament for Nottinghamshire on three separate occasions from 1673 until his death in 1713. During George I's reign he re-established the village of Langar which had become somewhat run down; the inn was built at this time with bricks from yards on his estate.

UNION

This name may commemorate the Union of England and Scotland in 1707 or the union of England and Ireland, 1801. It was also the name of a stagecoach.

Hinckley, Leicestershire. Has several apparitions; one is a man sitting at a table quietly reading a book until he simply fades away. The other is of a well-dressed 'highwayman' who may have frequented the pub or may have been hanged in the nearby market square, where all such punishments were carried out at the time.

Kelvedon, Essex. John Ayley, 1570-1636, the landlord, was brought before the leet – the manorial court – for a number of misdemeanours: failing to attend church or leaving early when he did, playing cards or dice, being drunk in sermon time, using scandalous language and obstructing the highway with a dunghill. Deemed to be 'a silly sort of fellow', he was treated leniently regarding these offences due to this position being 'necessary to the community' and his popularity as Mine Host.

There is no private house in which people can enjoy themselves
so well as at a capital tavern or inn.

Boswell's 'Life of Johnson', 1776

VALIANT TROOPER

Aldbury, Hertfordshire. Most buildings in the village are ancient, including this pub, which was originally three cottages. Supported by blackened rustic pillars, it has bare floorboards and whitewashed stone walls, with beer being served from a very small bar. The attached barn behind, now the dining hall, looks out on the garden.

First mentioned as an alehouse in 1752, when it was called the Royal Oak, a name it retained until 1803 when it became the Valiant Trooper Alehouse, supposedly after the Duke of Wellington visited to discuss tactics with his commanders.

VERNON ARMS

Admiral Vernon, 1684-1757, was the first to issue 'grog', a mixture of rum and water, in the British Navy. He was cashiered in 1746. Was his riddance drunk to by the sailors, I wonder?

Sudbury, Suffolk. When in 1659 George Vernon inherited, he wanted more than the small manor house and began building the Hall circa 1670, which was still being titivated in 1691. He demolished and rebuilt the village attached to the estate in 1671 and since it had to have an inn, its replacement was called the Vernon Arms.

VICTORIA

Many named after the nineteenth century queen, but it is also a four-wheeled carriage for two persons with folding top and raised seat for the driver.

Dunstable, Bedfordshire. A two-storey red-brick building with a coach entrance leading to a courtyard seating area. Has been a pub since at least the 1850s, but probably longer, as it has an arch for coaches, and Dunstable was an important stopping place on the Old Watling Street, the ancient road that went from Dover to Wroxeter. Since Roman times it has been a strategic crossroads with the Icknield Way that stretches from Norfolk to Wiltshire.

The swinging sign shows a full-length Queen Victoria in coronation robes with the Albert Hall over one shoulder, with possibly Osbourne House over the other, with a Victoria Cross Medal above. Complete Victoriana.

The pub has its ghost of a young stable lad who badly injured his hand; the rest of the story is rather vague, but whenever he appears one arm and the hand are bandaged.

There is another story concerning a witch called Sally who terrorised the town after her death. The frightened residents found a travelling priest who agreed to rid the town of Sally, but she put up a fight. In the end the priest cornered her then took hold of her shoulders and pushed her into a bottle, which he immediately sealed with a cork. He then buried the bottle under a cairn of stone in the graveyard with the warning that it should not be touched otherwise the witch would return once again to haunt the town. I remember an aunt who lived nearby taking me to the graveyard fruitlessly looking for the cairn after hearing the story, although I do recall finding gravestone dating from the 1700s.

Good ale, the true and proper drink of Englishmen. He is not deserving of the name of Englishman who speaketh against ale that is good ale.

From 'Lavengro', George Borrow.

WAGGON AND HORSES

Prior to the advent of the railway, most goods were moved by carters, and pubs were a convenient stopping place for these men, not just for sustenance but to collect and deliver other cargo, as many pubs acted as distribution points for either the village or the farms nearby. It was also a sign all in the countryside would know.

Ridge Hill, Hertfordshire. The first Trust House rented in 1904, who adopted the Hertfordshire County badge of the hart couchant as their logo.

An ex-policeman and his wife were appointed as managers with a salary of thirty shilling per week (£1.50p), excluding board for themselves and one servant. It was a popular cyclist's rest during the hey-day of cycling.

Stamford, Lincolnshire. It was here that Daniel Lambert, 1770-1809, was found dead in his room after having attended the races at Huntingdon. One of the world's fat men, he weighed three pounds under fifty-three stone, a suit of his clothes was displayed here. The inn was visited more than once by the 3' 4" American dwarf Charles Stratton – General Tom Thumb – who left a set of miniature clothes for comparison. Both sets are now in the Stamford Museum.

WALNUT TREES

Hedsor, Buckinghamshire. The parish boundary passes exactly through the building, so when the Beating the Bounds ceremony was enacted in times gone by, the beaters were convinced they could only do their duty properly by passing through the cellars of the inn – but remembering, of course, to have a suitable reviver en route. This would set them up for the future ordeal of having to ford the river in order to lay claim to a strip of land on the Berkshire side.

WATERCRESS HARRY

Kettering, Northamptonshire. Named after a local character, rumoured to be the disowned son of a parson who became a prize fighter for some time, in and around Leicester. He was later known in the Kettering area as a seller of watercress, oranges and home-made wreaths. Although of an unkempt appearance, he was well-spoken and polite. The name of the inn, originally the Gaiety Tavern, was changed in 1984.

WATTS ARMS

Hanslope, Buckinghamshire. The pub is a detached brick, Georgian cube building, with a symmetrical front façade featuring a central door, with three-sided bay window on either side supporting a portico over the front entrance. The first floor has two arches with recessed window and a third above the front entrance. The hanging sign shows the arms of the family.

Although the window tax was introduced in 1696, it was not repealed until 1851, so many buildings between those dates have bricked-up windows. This pub is one of them; it has a number of blind windows waiting to be glazed.

The Glaswegian boxer Alexander McKay, known as the Highland Hercules, was matched against Simon Byrne, the Emerald Gem, in a bare-knuckle fight for a purse of £200 each. Denied the right to fight outside the inn, the boxers and thousands of supporters crossed the county boundary into Northamptonshire, where magistrates were less obstructive to what was at that time an illegal but fanatically followed sport. So it was at Salcey Green that, after forty-seven rounds when McKay was beaten unconscious, he was taken back in a jolting carriage to the Watts Arms, where he later died.

He now haunts the pub, but until a fan of boxing history visited the pub and was told the story, no one knew who the ghost could be. From the description of the ghost he recognised who it was.

The pub is named after a local landowning family who incurred an unfortunate occurrence in 1912 when the gamekeeper murdered one of the family.

WELSH HARP

Waltham Abbey, Essex. Dates from the fifteenth century. There are two theories as to the origin of the pub name; years ago the Welsh drovers used to bring their cattle from Wales, where they were bred on the hills, to markets and fairs in England, where the prices they fetched were much higher. As droving was a solitary occupation, it is quite possible that some of these men would bring along their harps and other musical instruments to play during the long nights. Once they had sold the cattle, a drink would be needed and after a drink then… have you ever tried to stop a Welshman singing?

The other possibility was that a Welsh regiment was billeted close by, who in turn would use the pub with the same results as above.

WHEATSHEAF

Device on the arms of the Worshipful Company of Bakers, granted 1486 as well as on the arms of the Brewers' Company.

Daventry, Northamptonshire. The building is in the form of a great hollow square. The oldest part at the back began as a farmhouse in 1300. In a survey of the local manor made in Tudor times, the inn is mentioned as having been built in the thirteenth year of Queen Elizabeth I's reign, which would make the date 1571. A heavy cross bar which could be fitted into sockets across one of the old doors can still be seen and this was 'to protect the serving wenches' In former days, once the lads had tippled enough, something more than ordinary locks was needed. The door handles, too, had been heavily forged by a blacksmith.

Tradition has it that Charles I slept here before defeat at the Battle of Naseby and saw an apparition of Lord Strafford, whose death warrant he had felt compelled to sign some five years earlier. The ghost advised him to march north, saying the fight at Northampton was a battle he could not win. Charles stayed another day, by which time it was too late, as Fairfax's army was only a few miles away.

In the room where Charles once briefed his officers a rotary club now holds regular meetings; the panelling goes back to the Restoration. One of the treasures found was a large water colour on canvas discovered on the wall when layers of old wallpaper were stripped away. It has been estimated to be about three hundred years old.

There is an atmosphere about the place which builds up before midsummer, the critical time being June 6th, the date of King Charles I's arrival. Many people speak of sensations from the past which cannot be explained, and dogs definitely react to something only visible to them.

WHIFFLER

A whiffler was a member of a Corporation entourage who carried a 'wifel', which is a javelin, sword or staff which was used to clear a way through crowds so a procession could proceed. They were a regular part of these ceremonies in Norwich; the last time was on Guild Day in 1835, after which the custom seems to have lapsed.

Norwich, Norfolk. The pub is a large two-storey brick building with a red-tiled roof built in 1938. It is now one of a national chain. The decor inside has interesting illustration along with corresponding texts about Norwich.

The sign at the inn portrays the Whiffler in a rather splendid costume.

WHIP

Lacey Green, Buckinghamshire. The obvious meaning of the word is the instrument used to flog or beat someone or something, usually a handle with a flexible leather switch attached.

The sign shows a horseman urging his horse over a hedge. The hunting origins of the term comes from the whipper-in, the men who kept the hounds in order by the use of whips. They quickly became known as 'whips', a name perpetuated today in the House of Commons, where the whips keep straying MPs in order, much as their forefathers did with hounds. Some say there is not a lot of difference!

The pub, which is sited on the wonderfully named Pink Street, was for one short time called the Fiddlers Elbow, but there was such an outcry the brewery owners quickly changed it back. Power to the people!

Nearby the pub is the oldest smock mill still standing. Originally built at Chesham, it was moved here by the Duke of Buckingham.

WHITE HART

Many signs of a White Hart show the animal with a chain or crown round its neck, but exactly why seems to have been lost in the mists of time. One origin of a White Hart with a gold collar seems to have been mythical, as such animals seem to have extraordinary long lives and are supposed to be fairy animals that are never to be caught or are regarded as mystic beasts from the after world, so anyone who kills it is likely to suffer a dire fate.

One fable declares that Aristotle tells that Diomedes consecrated a white hart to Diana, which was killed some one thousand years later by Agathocles, King of Sicily. His fate is not recorded, although one source tells that he was poisoned by his son.

A further legend relates that Alexander the Great caught a white stag and placed a gold collar round its neck. This story so pleased ancient writers that they substituted Julius Caesar for Alexander and transplanted the story into Europe, where one was reputed to have been caught in Windsor Forest, another in Yorkshire, and others in France and Germany.

In English folklore a White Hart is associated with Herne the Hunter, which may be linked to the one in Windsor Forest.

A White Hart with a golden crown and chain is the badge of Richard II, son of the Black Prince, which was worn by his courtiers. It was adopted from his mother, Joan the fair Maid of Kent, whose cognisant was a white hind.

In Christian art it was the emblem of purity of life and solitude.

Just to show that such an animal is not totally a myth, one was photographed in the Cairngorms in Scotland during 2018. But without the gold chain!

Ampthill, Bedfordshire. The principal coaching house of the town. Built in Queen Anne-style with a brick façade from 1730, although some of the hotel is Tudor. An archway, not the accepted size for a coach, leads to a yard where there would have been stabling.

During restoration in 1975, a painting dating from 1646 was uncovered above an old fireplace showing the arms of Prince Charles, later King Charles II. A plaque on the wall beside the fire tells of its discovery. Also said to depict the Prince of Wales's feathers.

Suffered extensive damage to roof and upper floors due to an early-morning fire in 2000.

Chalfont St Peter, Buckinghamshire. This is another pub haunted by a previous landlord, Donald Ross. This one, though, is a merry old soul; he is heard dancing jigs to the sound of a violin, which he also plays. He is described as a middle-aged man who is light on his feet and with a happy smile. Sadly poor Donald died over a hundred years ago but still likes to get the customers on their feet.

Great Saling, Braintree, Essex. The inn stands on Stane Street at the junction of two Roman roads, so it is possible there was a tavern here during Roman times. The present is largely Tudor with moulded timber beams, the public bar having a giant log serving as a table, an open fire, flagstone floor and exposed wall timbers.

In the nineteenth century the inn did a great posting trade, and even as late as 1889 the landlord could provide a hundred horses at a push.

Remains of a once-open gallery can be seen in the yard, where the great joints of meat and game were hung to keep them fresh and was, even in the 1960s, the scene of a weekly egg and poultry market. The stabling and market have had to give way to a modern wing.

It was in the former bakery at the back of this pub that the local snack known as a 'huffer' originated, and the place is now renowned for this feather-light, three-cornered bap. At present the pub is closed awaiting its fate.

Hackleton, Northamptonshire. Claimed as the oldest hostelry in the village, the first recorded licensee was one Robert Holt in 1739.

The inn has a team belonging to the Northamptonshire Skittles League, a game involving wooden cheeses which are hurled at pins from a distance. These stand on a table with a net at the back and the hurler stands some seven feet away. All pretty noisy. These skittles can be found in other inns in the county.

Inside, suitably covered and a talking point in the bar, is an illuminated forty-foot-deep well which is still in use and supplies the pump outside.

Newark-on-Trent, Nottinghamshire. A fourteenth century inn and one of the oldest domestic buildings in the Midlands.

In 1619, Richard Cobbett stayed here with some Oxford friends.

Newmarket, Suffolk. The original inn was destroyed by a bomb during WWII, the new one having a strong racing flavour, as would be expected at the centre of English horse racing.

St Albans, Hertfordshire. Fifteenth century, dating back to 1430 and formerly the Hartshorn. One of England's finest and oldest half-timbered coaching inns set beside the abbey.

In 1746 Lord Lovat spent his last night in one of the beamed rooms before leaving for the Tower and his subsequent execution for treason. It was here Hogarth painted the portrait of him now in the National Portrait Gallery. The reproduction in the White Hart makes him look remarkably cheerful for a man about to take his last journey.

The Duke of Cumberland and Lady Grosvenor often stayed together at inns when travelling between London and Cheshire. He would disguise himself as a farmer in a black wig or appear as a young squire who was rather witless, thus becoming known as The Fool at various hostelries. It was at the White Hart that one of Lord Grosvenor's butlers broke down the door to discover the pair *in flagrante delicto.* It is not told what aroused his lordship's suspicions.

Haunted by Elizabeth Wilson, a young girl who was decapitated when the carriage she was travelling in sped under some arches, along with a past proprietor, who hanged himself in the cellar.

Warboys, Cambridgeshire. Haunted by victims of the plague who died at the inn when it reached the village in 1557. Also by Alice Samuel who, along with her husband John and daughter Agnes, were tortured at the inn trying to force an admission of witchcraft from them. They were all later hanged.

Part of the evidence used was the fact that Oliver Cromwell's grandmother had visited the three; she later became ill and died, which was blamed on witchcraft.

Ware, Hertfordshire. Reputedly the Great Bed of Ware was made for the inn as a publicity stunt about 1590; it was a massive four-poster, measuring about eleven feet square, and is reputed to sleep six couples. Must be extra friendly, though.

Weston Longville, Norfolk. Now unlicensed.

James Woodforde, a bachelor, educated at New College, Oxford, was rector in the village from 1776 till his death there in 1803 and is buried in the churchyard. Best known as Parson Woodforde, whose father was vicar at Castle Cary, Somerset.

His 'Diary of a Country Parson' in five volumes, ran from 1758 to 1802 and was published 1924-31.

WHITE HORSE

A white horse is a recognised Biblical symbol of victory. It is said the forces of Hengist and Horsa fought under the banner of a prancing white horse during the Jutish invasion of England in AD 449, still the device of the badge of Kent to this day. It was borne on the standard of the Anglo-Saxons and therefore impressed on hop pockets and bags as the traditional emblem of Kent.

It was also the symbol of the Kings of Wessex.

A rampant white horse is the device of the House of Savoy, descended from the Saxons.

The badge of a white horse, usually shown galloping, was bought into this country by the Hanoverian Kings and was associated with loyalty to the house of Hanover. The device dates from the accession of George I in 1714. During his reign and that of George II, the White Horse replaced the Royal Oak of Stuart fame on many public house signs.

The white horse was on Doggett's badge – to him it was a sign of freedom.

Also a military sign. The old 8th Foot, raised in 1685, now called the King's Liverpool Regiment, was called the White Horse from one of the badges – a white horse within the garter – and in 1716 the title was changed to 'The King's Regiment of Foot' at which time it was presented with the badge of the White Horse of Hanover.

The white horse also features in the arms of several guilds, including those of the carmen, coachmen, farriers, innholders, saddlers and wheelwrights.

Blythburgh, Suffolk. In 1750 a drunken black drummer, Tobias Gill, nicknamed Black Toby, from a Regiment of Dragoons, was convicted of raping and murdering a village girl, Anne Blakemore from Walberswick. He met the girl on the common when in a drunken stupor after visiting the inn. He was found lying next to her dead body but said he had not harmed her. There were no marks on her and no evidence she had been murdered, but nonetheless he was sentenced to death and his body later hung in chains at the crossroads. It is now thought she may have died of natural causes.

His ghost is supposed to haunt the heath, where he can be seen on a black hearse pulled by four black horses. Wraiths driving coaches with black headless horses represent those spirits doomed to Hell having been denied a Christian burial. Similar story as the Bell at Walberswick, Blyburgh, is close to Walberswick.

Anne's ghost has been reported running in front of cars before disappearing.

The pub was haunted by a little old man whom the landlord and his wife look upon as a monk. A lorry crashed through a wall of the house in 1967, killing the driver, and then the place was burgled followed by a fire, since when the ghost has been quieter! Never heard of a scared ghost before.

Gorleston, Norfolk. Famous as a rendezvous for smugglers. An ancient inn dating, some say, from the fourteenth century which became a ruin, so it was pulled down in 1893. The Gorleston smugglers had used the White Horse as their headquarters. When the house was being demolished, skeletons were found in an underground room which also contained an iron sea chest claimed to be the smugglers' 'bank' – but no note of what was inside.

At the time of Napoleon's threatened invasion of England a man claiming to be English resided at the inn. He was seen at all meetings and drills arranged in preparation for the proposed attack. He might not have raised suspicion but for the loose tongue of his companion, a young fisherman, who did not go unnoticed. Seized by the smugglers, after a search incriminating evidence was found among his possessions. The 'Smugglers' Court' was convened in the White Horse, and as the stranger's explanation was not satisfactory he was condemned as a spy and shot. A hundred or so years after, due to erosion of the cliff face, a coastguard on his beat saw a pair of jack boots protruding from the face of it. Once the discovery was known, people recalled the story of the spy who had been shot and buried there.

Kersey, Suffolk. White-rendered with tiled roof and an easy-to-read but rather dull sign.

This wool village gave its name to Kerseymere, a twilled cloth of fine wool, which is a corruption of cassimere, from cashmere.

Leiston, Suffolk. This hotel seems always to have been a free trader's rendezvous on a coast well known for the activity. Leiston, Westleton and the Eels Foot pub at Eastbridge are well documented as being associated with smuggling, despite having Dragoons billet at them.

The licensees in 1844 were a Mr and Mrs Gildersleeves. He is described as a brewer and spirit merchant; his wife – well known for her quick tongue and considerable resource – was also an infamous Leiston smuggler. One night the local Quakers were somewhat shocked at finding space under the platform at their meeting house had been used to store contraband liquor – not quite what they had had in mind!

Thurlton, Norfolk. This inn stood where the track across the marsh met the old turnpike.

In 1809, Joseph Bexfield, a wherryman, after having had a drink here, set out for home when he remembered he had left some items on the wherry tied up at the staithe and decided to pick them up. His cronies warned him that the Lantern Men, the name given to marsh lights, or Jack o' Lantern, were everywhere that night. Bexfield thought he knew the marsh well enough not to be led astray by them and off he went. Days later his body was washed up some distance away.

The White Horse is now Marsh Farm.

Welwyn Garden City, Hertfordshire. Welwyn was on the coach road to the north; it was called Welwin by the Saxons from its many springs.

The building is a four hundred-year-old coaching inn with open fires.

Edward Young, the vicar here, 1730-65, married the widowed grand-daughter of Charles II, Lady Elizabeth Lee, and bought Guessons/Guessens, the house opposite the church. Dr Johnson called there and met the vicar's son and his wife.

Westleton, Suffolk. Originally built of wattle and plaster with a thatched roof but rebuilt at the end of the nineteenth century. With smuggling and piracy being rife on this part of the coast, the inn was perfectly situated for involvement, and stories of ghosts abounded if only to keep people indoors at night.

WHITE LION

The badge of Edward IV as Earl of March; his supporters on the crest were a lion and antelope. He had inherited the symbol from his grandmother, Anne de Mortimer.

Device of the Dukes of Norfolk, statant gardent – standing facing the front. Also the badge of the Earl of Surrey, the Earl of Mortimer and the Fitz-Hammonds.

Walkern, Hertfordshire. In 1712, the judges and the witch finders stayed in this pub during one of the last witchcraft trials to be held in this country. By now it was getting hard to get a conviction for witchcraft after the previous century's purge by Matthew Hopkins, the self-proclaimed Witchfinder General.

Jane Wenham, a widow of the village, was the poor innocent who was being persecuted. She was found guilty and sentenced to be hanged, but later reprieved. For her own safety she was moved from the village to another part of Hertfordshire. It finally ceased to be a crime in 1736, although for some reason was left on the statute books.

In 1944 another woman was prosecuted under the witchcraft act. The woman Helen Duncan was a fake medium who told of the sinking of HMS *Barham* before it was publicly disclosed. This time it led to an investigation into her methods and ultimately a nine-month prison sentence, partly because the authorities were afraid she may disclose other sensitive information. The Act was finally repealed in 1951.

Warsop, Nottinghamshire. Thomas Smith was landlord here in 1722. He was a well-known local character and known as Tommy Tit, being full of pluck, although not a large man. One Sunday morning a traveller arrived at the inn and asked for a pint of ale. Tommy's wife served him and showed him into the parlour. On the fire a pot was simmering which contained the Sunday lunch. Later, when returning to check the progress of the meal, Tommy's wife discovered the dumpling, her husband's favourite delicacy, was missing from the pot. When Tommy heard this, he chased after the traveller who had quietly made off with it and set about him. A neighbour, wondering about this unequal fight, was told, "It is a poor dog who won't fight for his own dumpling" which became a proverbial saying thereabouts.

WHITE ROSE

Shakespeare, in *Henry VI* Part 1 Act 2 Scene 4, had the nobles of the opposing sides picking roses in the Temple Church to signify which side they supported.

However, the white rose was used as the badge of Richard, Duke of York, 1411-1460, and derived from his Mortimer ancestors. It was adopted by the Yorkists during the contest for the crown of England, which only became known as the Wars of the Roses after the publication of Sir Walter Scott's novel *Anne of Geierstein* in the nineteenth century. He took the idea from Shakespeare's play.

The red rose of Lancaster was chosen only after the battle of Bosworth Field in 1485.

It was also used by the Jacobins as an emblem of the Pretender, as his followers were obliged to speak of him *sub rosa*, i.e. in secret.

Other more unlikely contenders are The White Rose of Raby, who was Cecily, the wife of Richard Duke of York and mother of Edward IV and Richard III. Lady Catherine Gordon, given by James IV of Scotland as wife to Perkin Warbeck, was called this, as was Perkin Warbeck himself, being a Yorkist pretender to the throne.

On the overthrow of the Yorkists and the death of Richard, most White Rose inn signs were either painted red or had their name changed.

The white rose remains the Yorkshire emblem today.

WHITE SWAN

Dunstable, Bedfordshire. A two-storey cottage-type pub with whitewashed walls and a tiled roof that in past days would have catered for the many travellers who passed that way, as Dunstable is the meeting of old Roman roads that have been used over the centuries by those moving around the country. When sold in 1789 it was called the Two Black Boys; whether the name changed after the sale is not known. Perhaps it was named in the 1960s after the enamelled White Swan found during excavations of the old priory.

At one time part of the cellar was used as the town lock-up, complete with a grill to allow air in.

The pub has a ghost who does not show up on CCTV, despite being plainly seen by staff.

The swinging sign is plain white writing on a black background.

Gringley on the Hill, Nottinghamshire. The inn stands at Drakeholes, where the road crosses the Chesterfield canal, and was built by the landowner Jonathan Acklom sometime after 1771 to serve road and, later, water traffic.

WILD MAN

Norwich, Norfolk. This refers to Peter, a feral child found in Hanover in circa 1725 and brought to the English court by Queen Caroline of Ansbach. Interest was lost in him when he failed to learn to speak and he was put in the care of a farmer in Hertfordshire. Peter was a roamer however, and in 1751 having reached Norwich, was confined as a vagrant in the Bridewell. When it caught fire he was rescued and sent back to the farmer, who made him a collar, giving his address in case of further wandering. This collar can be seen in the Norwich School for Boys and his adventures remembered in Wild Man Hill, as well as the name of the pub. He may have died about 1785, but accounts vary.

The 'wild man' was usually a reference to the medieval wodewose, and until recently this Norwich sign showed a feathered savage. A novel of the late thirties written round the facts relates how Peter, as a baby, was stolen by a bear whose cub had died, and when his father came looking for him, she killed him. It is this story which appears on the inn's signboard today.

WINDMILL

Salthill, Slough, Buckinghamshire. The landlord and his wife, Mr and Mrs March, were described in 1781: "Her ugliness and notableness are as notorious as his cringing and cunning." He would always hobble forth, followed by a waiter bearing a tray of cakes and other delicacies hoping to ingratiate himself.

Edward Topham, 1751-1820, a journalist and playwright, wrote in 1826 that when he was at Eton, a boy in the sixth form was flogged for some misdemeanour which produced a rebellion among the other boys. Two hundred or so, instead of marching into school, ran across the playing fields and chucked their copies of Homer into the Thames. After this they all went down to the Windmill at Salthill. The landlord was a bit overwhelmed by this influx but did his best to provide for them. Accommodation was found, for most slept on the floor, and in the morning the reckoning was some hundred and fifty pounds. Recourse was to the Duke of Rutland and other boys of exalted rank, who were forced to pay up. The result was, five boys were expelled and the rest returned home to explain themselves.

WOOLPACK

Coggeshall, Essex. Previously called Woolpack and Punchbowl, situated in a former wool town, this timber-framed hostelry is older than 1500.

During the early nineteenth century it was another place where the townsfolk had a reputation for stupidity. One story tells they lit fires under plum trees to ripen the plums; another that when the town band was practising at the Woolpack, a passer-by came in and said how good they sounded from the street, at which all the band downed instruments and went outside to listen.

This swinging sign also shows a horse carrying a woolpack.

If all be true that I do think
There are five reasons we should drink:
Good wine, a friend, or being dry,
Or lest we should be by and by,
Or any other reason why.

Reasons for Drinking: Dean Aldrich, 1647-1710

YARBOROUGH ARMS

The title of Earl of Yarborough was created in 1837 for the 2nd Baron Yarborough. The family estate is at Brocklesby Park in North Lincolnshire, about ten miles east of Brigg.

Ulceby, Lincolnshire. A solid Georgian building. The family coat of arms is not only on the swinging sign but also on either side of the porch.

The 2nd Lord Yarborough used to lay a thousand pounds to one pound against a hand in bridge or whist being dealt that contained no card above a nine. This became known, and still is, as a Yarborough. His odds were a little out, as it is reckoned the true probability is 1,827 to one.

YARBOROUGH HUNT

The hunt takes the name from the Lord of the Manor who owns an estate at nearby Brocklesby.

Brigg, North Lincolnshire. A pub has stood on the site since the 1700s, having been built for the Earls of Yarborough. This pub was formerly the brewery tap for Sergeant's Brewery which closed in 1967, although the pub continued trading for a number of years after that under the auspices of several different breweries. There are two swinging signs. Alongside the old sergeant's sign of plain lettering with a large S in black in a white circle is the present one showing a member of the chase in hunting pink jumping his horse over a fence.

The horse and mule live for thirty years.
Yet know nothing of wines and beers.
The goat and sheep at twenty die.
Yet never get a taste of scotch or rye.
The cow drinks water by the ton.
And at eighteen is mostly done.
The dog at fifteen cashed in.
Without the aid of rum of gin.
The cat in milk and water soaks.
Then in twelve short years it surely croaks.
The modest sober bone dry hen.
Lays eggs for others then dies at ten.
All animals are strictly dry.
They sinless live yet swiftly die.
But sinful ginful rum soaked men.
Survive for three score and ten.
While some of us though very few.
Stays pickled 'til we're ninety two.

Anon.